Pathways

to

Academic English

4th Edition v2

Institute for Excellence in Higher Education, Tohoku University

Tohoku University Press, Sendai

Log in to our official website. Various online practice tools and worksheets are available to help you develop the skills outlined in this book.

www.pathwaystoacademicenglish.com

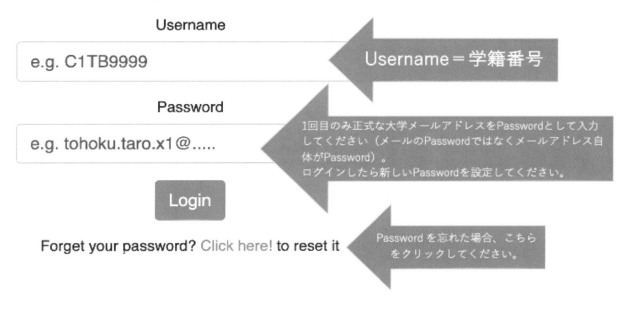

Pathways Login

Please fill in your credentials to login.

Username

e.g. C1TB9999

Username＝学籍番号

Password

e.g. tohoku.taro.x1@.....

1回目のみ正式な大学メールアドレスをPasswordとして入力してください（メールのPasswordではなくメールアドレス自体がPassword）。
ログインしたら新しいPasswordを設定してください。

Login

Forget your password? Click here! to reset it

Password を忘れた場合、こちらをクリックしてください。

What's inside the website?

他の学生と切磋琢磨する！

Password 変更、学習進捗の確認など

Multimodal
Flashcards
Worksheets
Tools

Pathways to Academic English

Student Pathways   Our Missions   Log Out

LEADERBOARD

MY PAGE

MESSAGES
Hello ABCD1234

英語教育に関する連絡

I・A   I・B

II・A   II・B

English III

前期の Online Tools

後期の Online Tools

2年生の Online Tools

Pathways to Academic English 4th Edition v2

Table of Contents

English II-A: Integrated Academic Reading and Writing

1. *Identify the text's organization and logic*

2. *Construct an academic paragraph*

English II-B: Integrated Academic Speaking and Listening

1. *Understand a speaker's intent*

2. *Discuss academic topics*

序文

研究大学である東北大学では、学部を問わず、working language（共通使用言語）として英語が使われています。したがって、学生の皆さんは専門領域の知識や教養を身に付ける際、英語を通じて知識を取り入れ、英語を使って考察・発表・執筆する機会を持つこととなります。このような学術目的の英語の土台を作るために提供されるのが、全学教育として英語科目（1・2年次）です。

本書は、入学生向け英語カリキュラムに準拠した共通教材として、学術英語の土台として必要なCore Skills を解説したものです。1年次では4つの英語科目（「英語 I-A」「英語 I-B」「英語 II-A」「英語 II-B」）を履修することになりますが、各科目には Core Skills が4つずつ配置されています。担当教員は、この4つの Core Skills を全て取り入れた授業を行い、学生が本書の内容を習得できるよう練習を重ねます。2年次では、1年次で学習した16の Core Skills を踏まえて、アカデミックプレゼンテーションなどに取り組みます。ある題材について、考えや情報を論理的に構造化し、効果的に伝える方法を学びます。

これらの Core Skills が、学部高年次における専門科目や大学院での本格的な研究に従事する際の一般的基礎力となるので、手を抜くことなく英語力の一層の向上に励んでください。また、本書に収められた16の Core Skills は学術目的ですが、将来の活躍の場所を官公庁や企業、あるいは起業に求める人にとっても有益なスキルとなるでしょう。なぜなら、どのような進路を選ぶにしても、それぞれの分野における専門性を身に付けることが求められるからです。

本書はこの「序文」を除き、すべて英語で書かれていますが、これには理由があります。すでに述べたとおり、英語を通じて専門分野の知識や幅広い教養を身に付けていくことが、これから皆さんに求められる英語との付き合い方です。したがって、学術目的の英語力を身に付けるのも英語を通じて行ってほしいと願うからです。実際、本学では多くの英語科目が英語で実施されることになるでしょう。

英語は履修科目の1つというよりは、研究・学習のための道具であり、環境です。学生の皆さんがすでに習得している英語力を向上させ、英語を working language として駆使できるよう、本書がその一助となることを願ってやみません。

Tips for Improving Your General Academic English Skills

1. ## <u>Use the online tools!</u>

   These allow you to practice reading, listening, speaking, and writing. You need to learn the information in this book, but you require more practice than just reading the book. The more you use the tools, the more you will improve your English!

2. ## <u>Use a variety of tools and practice types!</u>

   We have found that students who do a variety of practice (reading, listening, speaking, and writing) improve more than those who only practice reading or multiple-choice questions. Every chapter has at least one online tool for practice.

   🔊 The audio files for B chapter examples can also be found on the webpage.

3. ## <u>Use the vocabulary, phrases, and expressions in this book!</u>

   The vocabulary, phrases, and expressions have been carefully selected; practice using them in class and with the online tools. Notice that the online tools match the tables and charts in this book.

4. ## <u>Use English as much as possible!</u>

   There are many chances to read, write, speak, and listen to English on campus. Utilize the resources such as the library and student learning advisers.

English I-A
Academic Reading and Vocabulary

Objective 1: Improve reading and vocabulary-building skills

1. Word Parts

2. Synonym Vocabulary

Objective 2: Recognize the text's main idea, key information, and gist

3. Skimming and Scanning

4. Paraphrasing and Summarizing

1. Word Parts

Many medical, legal, scientific, and technical words in English are made up of Latin and Greek word parts, though some may have origins from other languages. Students who are familiar with word parts can more easily:

1. reinforce their understanding of known words
2. anticipate the meanings of unknown words
3. identify the part of speech of a word

Therefore, learning the meanings and functions of the word parts found in the lists below will allow students to accelerate their vocabulary building skills and improve both their reading speed and comprehension.

There are three basic types of English word parts: **prefixes**, **roots**, and **suffixes**. Though there are various word formation patterns, the *prefix-root-suffix* pattern is common.

> Learning prefixes and suffixes, and how they affect meaning when they are added to simple roots can accelerate vocabulary building, which in turn, will improve your reading ability.

Prefixes

Prefixes come at the beginnings of words. They usually have clear meanings. However, though two prefixes may have the same meaning, they may have different usages and nuances. For example, the Latin prefix *multi-* and the Greek prefix *poly-* both mean *many*. However, the adjective *multicultural* refers to the practice of several human cultures existing in the same society at the same time. In contrast, the noun *polyculture* refers to the practice of growing several crops in the same area at the same time. Therefore, it is important to pay close attention to how the word parts are used in example vocabulary. Table 1 presents a list of common English prefixes, their meanings, and example vocabulary.

Table 1. Common Prefixes in English

	Prefix(es)	**Meanings**	**Example Vocabulary**
1	a-, non-	without	apathy, nontoxic, nonsense
2	anti-, contra-	against, opposing	contradiction, antisocial
3	ad-, at-	towards	attract, advance

	Prefix(es)	Meanings	Example Vocabulary
4	auto-	self	automatic, autograph
5	circum-, peri-	around	circumstance, perimeter
6	co-, syn-	with	cooperate, synchronize
7	de-	removing, down	deforest, defrost
8	dis-, un-	not, away	dishonest, disallow, discard, uncaring
9	en-/em-	adding, entering	entrap, empower
10	ex-	out, former	exit, extract
11	hemi-, semi-	half, partial	hemisphere, semicircle, semipro
12	hyper-, over-	too much	hypertension, over-extend
13	in-/im-/il-/ir-	not, non	injustice, illogical
14	inter-	between	international, intercept
15	mal-, mis-	wrong, bad, sick	malicious, misinterpret
16	meta, trans	through, across	metaphor, translate
17	mono-, uni-	one	monopoly, uniform
18	multi-, poly-	many	polyglot, multimedia
19	post-	after	postscript, postmodern
20	pre-	before	predict, preview
21	pro-	forward, giving	promote, provide
22	re-	back, again	reuse, retreat
23	sub-	under	subway, subconscious
24	super-	above, better	superior, superscript
25	tele-	afar	telescope, telephone

Roots

Roots can come at any place within a word and usually have distinct meanings. Knowing these meanings is helpful when reading academic texts because Latin and Greek word roots are often used in science, engineering, and medical terms. Additionally, when new words are created, or new technology is invented, Latin and Greek roots are often used to create the new English word. For example, the word *telephone* was created by combining the Greek prefix *tele* (distant) and the root *phon* (sound).

Identifying Latin and Greek word parts, particularly those found in the tables of commonly occurring word parts, will especially benefit students whose majors are engineering, medicine, and science. Using resources such as etymology (word origin) dictionaries can help increase vocabulary building and knowledge of technical terms.

Usually, but not always, Greek word parts combine with other Greek word parts and Latin word parts combine with other Latin word parts. For example, consider the words *monochrome* and *uniform* below.

Prefix	Origin	Meaning	Root	Origin	Meaning
mono-	Greek	one	*chrome*	Greek	one color
uni-	Latin		*form*	Latin	one pattern

Other examples include:

Greek: monograph, monopoly, monotonous
Latin: unification, united, universal

The spellings of most word parts of Latin origin seem to match their pronunciations. However, word parts of Greek often have spellings that do not seem to match their pronunciations. Learning some of the Greek spelling and pronunciation conventions below will help you to remember the spellings and pronunciations of many academic words.

Be aware of the following conventions found in many Greek word parts:
1. The letter *f* and the *f* sound are usually spelled *ph* (e.g., **ph**otogra**ph**)
2. The letter *i* as a short vowel is sometimes spelled *y* (e.g., m**y**th, s**y**mpathy)
3. The letter *g* without other consonants is often pronounced *j* (e.g., **g**eography, **g**enerate)
4. The letter *p* at the beginning of a word is often silent (e.g., **p**seudo, **p**neumonia)
5. The *ch* combination is usually pronounced *k* (e.g., **ch**rome, **ch**emistry)

Table 2 presents a list of common roots, their meanings, and example vocabulary.

Table 2. Common Roots in English

	Root(s)	Meanings	Example Vocabulary
1	bi, di	two	bicycle, diode
2	tri	three	tricycle, triangle
3	qua(r)t, tetra	four	quarter, tetrapod
4	quint, pent	five	quintuplet, pentagon
5	anim, bio	living	animal, biological
6	aqua, hydro	water	aquatic, hydrogen
7	agri	field	agriculture, agribusiness
8	astro	star	asterisk, astronaut
9	capt/cept	catch	capture, intercept
10	corp, phys	body	corpse, physical, physician
11	cred	believe	credit card, incredible

	Root(s)	Meanings	Example Vocabulary
12	dict	say, word	dictionary, predict
13	dom, eco	home, environment	domestic, ecosystem
14	duc(t)	guide, gather	conduct, produce
15	dur	hard, last	duration, durable, endure
16	equ, homo	same	equal, homogeneous
17	flect(x)	bend	flexible, reflect
18	form, morph	shape	uniform, metamorphosis
19	herb, botan	plant	herbicide, botany
20	hemo	blood	hemoglobin, hemorrhage
21	hetero	different	heterogeneous, heterosexual
22	homin, anthrop	human	hominoid, anthropology
23	ign, pyr	fire	ignite, pyrophoric
24	ject	throw	object, eject
25	lact	milk	lactate, lactic acid
26	ling, lang	tongue, language	bilingual, language
27	loc	place, position	location, local
28	log	study, reasoning	logic, biology
29	lum(in), phot	light	illumination, photosynthesis
30	max, macro	large	maximum, macroeconomics
31	ment, psych(o)	mind, soul	mental, psychology
32	meter	measure	metric, kilometer
33	mini, micro	small	miniature, microscope
34	mort, necr	death	mortal, necrophobia
35	nat/nai/nasc, gen	birth	generate, genre, native, natal
36	nov, neo	new	novel, innovate, neoliberal
37	omni, pan	all	omnibus, panorama
38	path	suffering, feeling	pathology, sympathy, pathetic
39	ped, pod	foot	pedal, tripod
40	pel	push	repel, expel
41	pend	hang	depend, suspend
42	port	carry	portable, export
43	rupt	break	rupture, erupt
44	scribe, script, graph	record, write	prescribe, graphic
45	sol, heli	sun	parasol, helium
46	sol	alone	solo, desolate
47	son, phon	sound	sonic, phonology
48	spec	look, characteristic	special, inspect

	Root(s)	Meanings	Example Vocabulary
49	tempor, chron	time	temporal, chronological
50	terr, geo	ground, earth	territory, geography
51	therm	heat	thermometer, thermal
52	tract	pull	tractor, distract
53	vac	empty	vacant, evacuate
54	vert	turn, change	vertical, convert, invert
55	vis, scope	see	visual, microscope

Suffixes

Unlike prefixes and roots, Latin and Greek **suffixes** do not always have distinct meanings in English. Rather, they generally form the part of speech of a word (i.e., noun, verb, adjective, or adverb). Recognizing the final suffix of a word helps you to instantly identify the part of speech of a word.

Language in Action:

Consider the following sentences that use a form of the word *judge*. Notice the final suffix attached to the word in each.

Sentence	Final Suffix	Part of Speech
He **judged** the competition fairly.	N/A	verb
The final **judgment** of his thesis finished on time.	-ment	noun
The reviewers of my paper were very **judgmental**.	-al	adjective
She stared at him **judgmentally** while he worked.	-ly	adverb

Mastering suffix usage is important for paraphrasing (see Chapter 4) and enables you to avoid common part of speech grammatical errors.

Table 3 presents a list of common suffixes, their meanings, and example vocabulary.

Table 3. Common Suffixes in English

	Suffix	Attaches to a	Forms a	Meanings	Example Vocabulary
1	-ate	noun	verb	to do (～)	facilitate, accentuate
2	-en	adjective		to make (～)	sweeten, brighten
3	-ify	adjective		to make (～)	purify, solidify
4	-ize	noun/adj		to do (～)	prioritize, summarize

	Suffix	Attaches to a	Forms a	Meanings	Example Vocabulary
5	-ance	verb	noun	the action of (〜)	performance, allowance
6	-(m)ent	verb		the effect of doing (〜)	government, judgment
7	-(t)ion	verb		the result of doing (〜)	imagination, succession
8	-ant	verb		person doing (〜)	assistant, immigrant
9	-er/-or	verb		person doing (〜)	teacher, operator
10	-ist	noun		person doing (〜)	guitarist, nutritionist
11	-oid	noun		the shape of (〜)	humanoid, android
12	-ness	adjective		the degree of (〜)	darkness, sweetness
13	-ity	various		the degree of (〜)	acidity, ability
14	-hood	various		time/place of (〜)	childhood, neighborhood
15	-ism	various		theory of (〜)	pacifism, optimism
16	-phile	various		person loving (〜)	anglophile, xenophile
17	-phobe	various		person who fears (〜)	xenophobe, technophobe
18	-phobia	various		condition of fearing (〜)	acrophobia, hydrophobia
19	-able	verbs	adjective	capable of (〜)	enjoyable, readable
20	-al	noun		characteristic of (〜)	judgmental, experimental
21	-ic	noun			historic, heroic
22	-y	noun			windy, dirty
23	-ous	noun			poisonous, famous
24	-ive	noun		function/tendency of (〜)	expensive, supportive
25	-ese/-an	noun		originated from (〜)	Japanese, Mexican
26	-ful	noun		characterized by (〜)	eventful, forgetful
27	-less	noun		without (〜)	careless, sugarless
28	-ish	noun		like / belonging to (〜)	childish, boyish
29	-ly	noun		having qualities of (〜)	friendly, motherly
30	-ly	adjective	adverb	the way of / do like (〜)	wisely, colorfully

Comprehensive Example

Read the passage below and choose the word that best fills in each blank.

In order to find the answers to the questions, use the information about word parts and tables of word parts presented in this chapter.

Reading Passage

Scientists ___ (1) ___ animals according to their characteristics. These decisions are based primarily on ___ (2) ___, i.e., the shapes of structures in the animal's body, and developmental characteristics, such as body plan. However, habitat is not considered, so whether an animal lives on land or is ___ (3) ___, is far less important than whether the animal has a spine, contains a gut, or exhibits body symmetry.

1) Which word best fits in blank __(1)__?
   (A) class
   (B) classy
   (C) classify
   (D) classification

2) Which word best fits in blank __(2)__?
   (A) credibility
   (B) durably
   (C) animality
   (D) morphology

3) Which word best fits in blank __(3)__?
   (A) aquatic
   (B) geological
   (C) botanical
   (D) mortal

See Page 121 for Answers

2. Synonym Vocabulary

A **synonym** is a word or phrase that has exactly or nearly the same meaning as another word or phrase. Increasing vocabulary is important for improving all language skills, and synonym vocabulary knowledge is especially useful when paraphrasing and summarizing (see Chapter 4). However, good writers must make synonym vocabulary choices based on context.

> Reviewing the list of common synonyms in Table 1 can accelerate vocabulary building. The best way to remember new vocabulary is by putting them into practice. This means studying them by their collocations and in different contexts. Be aware that many words may have several meanings and the nuance may vary depending on the context. Therefore, synonyms are not always interchangeable.

Word part knowledge (see Chapter 1) can increase synonym vocabulary knowledge. Learning **word families** (combinations of the word and common prefixes and suffixes) enables students to recognize synonyms in their different forms and parts of speech.

> Also be aware of **homonyms** and **antonyms**. Homonyms are words that have the same spelling or pronunciation but different meanings, such as the noun *bear* (the animal) and the verb *bear* (to endure). Antonyms are different words that have opposite meanings. Many antonyms can be formed simply by adding a prefix, such as *usual* and *unusual*, or *advantage* and *disadvantage*.

Table 1. List of Common Academic Synonyms

	Synonym 1	Synonym 2	In Context
1	aesthetically	artistically	The architect designed the building more (synonym) than functionally.
2	allegedly	supposedly	There are studies (synonym) showing that this treatment works.
3	appellation	moniker	Elvis earned the (synonym) "The King" due to his popularity.
4	archetype	model	Pluto is the perfect (synonym) of a dwarf planet.
5	assembling	gathering	The research team will be (synonym) in the laboratory at 9:00.
6	blurry	indistinct	His image was (synonym) due to the poor Wi-Fi connection.

	Synonym 1	**Synonym 2**	**In Context**
7	bound	tied	An electron is (synonym) to a nucleus by electromagnetism.
8	common	widespread	The chemical formula for water, H_2O, is (synonym) knowledge.
9	concoction	combination	This (synonym) of chemicals is toxic.
10	conserve	retain	It is important to (synonym) resources after natural disasters.
11	counteracted	negated	Her new policies completely (synonym) the previous rules.
12	devote	dedicate	Rare individuals (synonym) their lives to the service of others.
13	displayed	shown	Your permit must be (synonym) at the entrance gate.
14	drawbacks	problems	His proposal has too many (synonym) for us to proceed.
15	emanating	radiating	This device is used to detect light (synonym) from distant stars.
16	employed	used	We (synonym) a novel technique to gather the relevant data.
17	enclosing	surrounding	A fence was built (synonym) the flower garden.
18	enhance	improve	Although her speaking ability is already good, she still practices every day to (synonym) it.
19	envisioned	imagined	The project was completed just as I (synonym), so it was a success.
20	fad	trend	Brightly dyed hair has become a (synonym) among teenagers.
21	forage	search	Wild chimps (synonym) for food for up to 18 hours a day.
22	holistic	comprehensive	Deep learning requires a (synonym) teaching approach.
23	illuminated	clarified	His lecture (synonym) the more difficult parts of the textbook.
24	infamous	notorious	She was (synonym) for continuously ignoring company rules.
25	lethal	deadly	Surprisingly, tarantula venom is not (synonym) to humans.
26	lineage	ancestry	Most people do not know much about their (synonym) beyond their immediate family.

	Synonym 1	**Synonym 2**	**In Context**
27	magnified	intensified	Scrutiny of the data will be (synonym) once it is published.
28	medium	means	Metal wire is used as a (synonym) to conduct electricity.
29	minimizes	reduces	It is known that physical exercise (synonym) mental stress.
30	objective	purpose	To succeed in your studies, you must have a clear (synonym).
31	obligation	duty	Parents have a(n) (synonym) to provide for their children.
32	obvious	apparent	Subatomic particles have no (synonym) physical structure.
33	peculiar	unusual	The bacteria have a very (synonym) knot-like protein structure.
34	period	phase	Picasso went through a (synonym) using only bluish paints.
35	pertain	relate	The old professor often talks about things that do not (synonym) to the subject of the class.
36	previous	former	He comes highly recommended by his (synonym) employer.
37	resume	restart	We hope to (synonym) the game as soon as possible.
38	salvaged	saved	I think the data can be (synonym) if we act quickly.
39	strata	layers	The Grand Canyon is made up of over 40 rock (synonym).
40	suggest	imply	The results (synonym) that our presumptions were correct.
41	symmetrical	balanced	A normal distribution is called a bell curve because the (synonym) shape of the graph resembles a bell.
42	alter	change	The new evidence did not (synonym) public opinion at all.
43	ubiquitous	prevalent	Toyotas are the most (synonym) vehicle on the road today.
44	witnessed	observed	The crime was not (synonym) by anyone.
45	zealots	fanatics	Though common in the 1970s, political (synonym) are rare today.
46	null	void	The contract is (synonym) if either party violates the agreement.

	Synonym 1	Synonym 2	In Context
47	fervent	ardent	His (synonym) supporters marched with him to city hall.
48	infraction	violation	A minor traffic (synonym) can have serious consequences.
49	inflict	wreak	Luckily, the typhoon did not (synonym) havoc on the town.
50	robust	strong	The economy remained (synonym) throughout the 1980s.
51	animosity	hatred	The heated disagreement caused (synonym) between them.
52	hurl	sling	The debate ended when he began to (synonym) insults at others.
53	anxious	nervous	It is hard not to feel a little (synonym) when meeting someone new.
54	deplete	exhaust	Action must be taken soon not to (synonym) the earth's resources.
55	cite	quote	If you (synonym) another author's research, you must acknowledge them in your reference list.
56	chaotic	disorderly	The meeting was very (synonym), so little was accomplished.
57	clemency	leniency	The lawyer sought (synonym) for his client.
58	freight	cargo	Three percent of the world's (synonym) is carried through the Panama Canal.
59	mitigate	alleviate	The medicine, though very effective, does not entirely (synonym) pain.
60	concurrent	simultaneous	(synonym) studies will be conducted in three different countries.

Context

Some words are only synonyms in particular contexts. Always check context before selecting a synonym.

Language in Action:

The first step to comprehension is determining the correct meaning of a word in a sentence. For example, the word *great* means *very large* but also *excellent*. Its synonym, *immense*, has only the meaning *very large* but never *excellent*. Read the following sentences and notice how the word *great* is used.

1. The amount of power used to operate an air conditioning unit is so **great** that electricity usage in summer outweighs that of winter.
2. His final report on electromagnets was so **great** that our professor used it as an example of a good report in his future classes.

Sentence 1: *immense* can be used to replace *great*
Sentence 2: *exceptional* or *excellent* can replace *great*, but *immense* cannot

Even though words may have similar meanings, most have different connotations (see Chapter 9), nuances, or usage (see Chapter 11) and only make sense in particular situations. If two words have similar meanings, they might only be acceptable replacements in certain contexts. Look at the sentences below and use this knowledge to ascertain the meaning of the words *forage* and *search*.

3. During spring, when flowers are blooming, worker bees are often sent away from the hive in order to **forage** for food.
4. Unfortunately, his advisor moved to a different university before he finished his dissertation, so he had to **search** for a new advising professor.

Sentence 3: *Forage* and *search* have similar meanings and can be used interchangeably in the contexts of *foraging* or *searching* for food. Using *forage* evokes a sense of desperation for food, mostly associated with animals.
Sentence 4: *Forage* is not an appropriate replacement in this context, where *search* has a meaning closer to *look for*. Such differences in nuance are often due to the connotative meaning of words (see Chapter 9).

Similarly, sometimes synonyms cannot be used if a word is being used in a set expression, such as a collocation (see Chapter 11) or idiomatic expression (see Chapter 7). For example, though *doubt* and *mistrust* are synonyms, *doubt* is part of the set phrase *cast doubt on*, and therefore *mistrust* cannot replace *doubt* in the sentence below.

Recent research in the field of evolutionary biology has cast **doubt** on the idea that all changes in species occur over an extended period of time.

Take the following steps in order to correctly choose a synonym in context:

1. Carefully read the surrounding words in the text.
2. Consider the possibility that a word might have multiple meanings. If it does, determine which meaning is being used based on the surrounding text.
3. Notice if the surrounding text provides a certain feeling or connotation. Choose a synonym that matches the intended meaning of the text.
4. Check if the word is being used in a set expression. If it is, choose a synonym that can also be used in the same set of words.

Word Parts and Word Families

Word part knowledge will help students identify synonyms and use them correctly. Identifying prefixes, roots, and suffixes can clarify the meaning of words, and help you to find a similar word created from different word parts.

You may recall from Chapter 1 that English acquired many word parts with similar meanings from different languages. Sometimes synonyms can be found simply by replacing Latinate word parts with Greek word parts, or an English word with similar meaning.

Language in Action:

Look at the sentences below and notice how synonyms can be found for *psychological* and *incredible* by considering the meanings of the word parts in each word.

1. I am taking Dr. Young's class about **psychological** disorders.
2. He achieved **incredible** results by changing his methodology.

Greek Word Part	Suffix	Latin Word Part	Suffix	Synonym
psych	-al	ment	-al	mental

Prefix	Latin Word Part	Suffix	Prefix	English Word	Suffix	Synonym
in-	cred	-ble	un-	believe	-able	unbelievable

3. I am taking Dr. Young's class about **mental** disorders.
4. He achieved **unbelievable** results by changing his methodology.

Knowledge of suffixes can assist in using synonyms correctly. When replacing one word with another, the part of speech should be consistent, and therefore, the suffix of a potential synonym should be modified accordingly. For example, the word *psychology* cannot replace *mental* in sentence 3, because *psychology* is a noun, but *mental* is an adjective. However, adding the suffix *-al* to *psychology* makes it an appropriate synonym, as in sentence 1.

Synonym knowledge can be greatly increased by learning word families – groups of words that contain the same root and basic meaning, but different suffixes or prefixes.

For example, consider the word family for *consist*.

+ency (n)	+ent (adj)	+ly (adv)	in+, +ency (n)	in+, +ent (adj)	in+, +ly (adv)
consistency	consistent	consistently	inconsistency	inconsistent	inconsistently

Knowing the word family for *consist* allows you to quickly realize that the following sentences have the same basic meanings: *this sample is not consistent* is *this sample is inconsistent*; *this sample lacks consistency*; *this sample has inconsistencies*. Furthermore, if you have knowledge of word families and know that *consistent* and *constant* are synonyms, you should be able to realize that *consistently* and *constantly* are also synonyms.

Comprehensive Example

Read the passage below and answer the questions based on the information presented in this chapter.

Reading Passage

Symbiosis refers to any long-term biological interaction between two different species. There are three types of symbiosis: mutualism, commensalism, and parasitism. Mutualistic symbiosis is defined as a relationship that **improves** the conditions of both species. For example, the bacteria that live in the guts of many herbivores help them to digest their food, and in turn receive a safe place to live. Commensalism is a relationship in which one species benefits, and there are no **drawbacks** for the other species. One example is a spider building a web on a plant – the plant provides a home for the spider, but the spider does not help or harm the plant in any way. The last type of symbiosis is parasitism, and it is by far the most **asymmetrical**. In a parasitic relationship, one species is harmed while the other prospers. Usually, the benefiting species is not **lethal** to the other species, but will often **inflict** havoc on the impaired species.

1) The word *improves* is closest in meaning to:

    (A) wins

    (B) enhances

    (C) observes

    (D) benefits

2) The word *drawbacks* is closest in meaning to:

    (A) rejections

    (B) layers

    (C) problems

    (D) limitations

3) The word *asymmetrical* is closest in meaning to:

    (A) unbalanced

    (B) fanatical

    (C) peculiar

    (D) animosity

4) The word *lethal* is closest in meaning to:

    (A) toxic

    (B) deadly

    (C) ubiquitous

    (D) holistic

5) The word *inflict* is closest in meaning to:

    (A) negate

    (B) retain

    (C) imply

    (D) wreak

See Page 121 for Answers

3. Skimming and Scanning

Skimming and **scanning** are techniques that are used to obtain information from a long text quickly and efficiently. When skimming, readers identify **keywords** and get the main idea of the text. When scanning, readers find **specific information** by swiftly searching for keywords and phrases and then carefully read the surrounding text.

> Skimming and scanning are especially important when conducting background reading for research projects. Many third year, fourth year, and graduate courses require students to obtain a lot of information from written texts in a short time. Additionally, skimming and scanning are essential when taking standardized English tests.

In order to **skim**, rapidly look over the pages and pay close attention to prominent features such as tables, charts, headings, numbered lists, bold text, italic text, parenthetical text, dates, names, and numbers. If you notice that any words or phrases are repeated in these features, you should regard them as a keyword, which can later be used for scanning.

When skimming, read the first and last sentences of each paragraph because these often include the main idea of the paragraph. You can understand what the text is mostly about by determining the main ideas of each paragraph.

> It is a good idea to take notes about keywords and main ideas when skimming. You should also highlight any potentially important information.

In order to **scan**, you must first have some specific information that you are looking for. For example, if you are scanning a research paper, you might only be looking for the results of the experiment, or how it was conducted. Similarly, on a reading test, you will only look for the information that will help you to answer a question.

When scanning, physically point out and highlight (or circle) keywords, which can be determined either by skimming, or by finding important words in questions or additional materials.

While scanning, you can usually ignore all other words until you come across a keyword. At this point, you must stop and carefully read the text surrounding the keyword or phrase thoroughly. When possible, you should look up unknown words and highlight sentences that contain information related to the keywords.

The idea of not reading every word in a text may make some readers feel uncomfortable at first—especially during examinations. However, these skills are critical for academic reading, so they must be practiced regularly.

Comprehensive Example

Below is a reading passage with several comprehension questions similar to a standardized English test. Practice by doing the following:

1. Skim the reading passage and identify the main idea of the passage and some keywords and phrases. _Do not_ read the entire passage.
2. Read the comprehension questions at the end of the passage and highlight keywords and phrases.
3. Use scanning to look for the keywords in the passage, then read the surrounding text carefully to find the answer to each question.
4. Answer the comprehension questions.

Reading Passage

One of the most notable groups of Native Americans in the United States is the Sioux. However, the word _Sioux_ actually refers to a large group of many different Native American tribes, which can be further classified into sub-groups. The first categorization is made based on language division – one group speaks **Dakota**, and the other speaks **Lakota**. Within the Dakota people, there is one more classification generally created based on where they live. The _Eastern Dakota_ reside mostly in the U.S. states of Minnesota, Iowa, and South Dakota, whereas the _Western Dakota_ mostly live in Montana, Wyoming, and the western parts of North Dakota. Similarly, there are further divisions within the Lakota people, which consist of seven bands or sub-tribes. This classification system is exhibited in the figure below.

Figure 1. _Classification of Sioux Sub-groups_

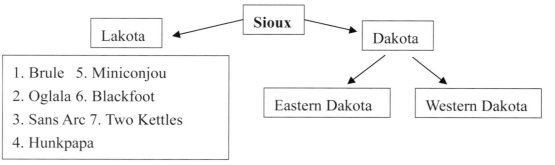

History

As the Sioux did not keep written records, not much is known about their history before interaction with Europeans in the late seventeenth century. However, based on archeological evidence and traditional lore passed down through the Sioux people themselves, it seems that their ancestors most likely began living in the Minnesota and Wisconsin areas around 1200 years ago, and created their tribal society around 1300 AD.

In the early eighteenth century, the Dakota were angered by the Europeans trading with other Native American tribes, who were the enemies of the Sioux. This led to a war between the Sioux and other tribes which lasted from 1720 until 1736, and resulted in the Dakota losing many of their traditional lands. After several continued wars that lasted until the late eighteenth century, many of the Sioux people began to move further west into the plainlands that have since become the U.S. states of North and South Dakota.

After moving, the Dakota signed their first treaty with the United States government in 1805. More tribes signed agreements with the United States and this brought peace to the area until **The Dakota War of 1862**, which was caused by a delay in the agreed payment to the Sioux people. The Dakota, led by *Little Crow*, were victorious in the first battle, but soon surrendered about a month later. As a result of the war, the U.S. government suspended all treaty rights to the Dakota and forced them to forfeit their lands. This only raised tensions, which resulted in many more wars and battles between all Sioux people and the United States, including *Red Cloud's War* (1866–1868), *The Great Sioux War of 1876*, *The Black Hills War* (1876–1877), *The Battle of Little Bighorn* (1876), and *The Wounded Knee Massacre* (1890).

From the 1890s to 1930s, the Dakota and Lakota tribes were divided and sent to live on assigned pieces of land called reservations. During this time, many of the people in these tribes were forced to adapt more European ways of life. From the 1930s to 1960s, the U.S. government changed its policy towards Native Americans and allowed them to reestablish communities, including their own constitutions and systems of governments within reservations. Though tensions with the United States in general have lessened, many Sioux people are still fighting for tribal rights, self-determination, and for particular lands to be returned to them.

Famous Figures

One of the most famous Sioux figures was Sitting Bull, a Hunkpapa Lakota leader who resisted the United States in the late nineteenth century, taking part in several wars.

Though he was not involved in the initial conflicts, such as the Dakota War of 1862, Sitting Bull helped defend his people from retaliatory attacks by the U.S. Army, and then joined his people in fighting Red Cloud's War and the Great Sioux War of 1876. Sitting Bull eventually surrendered himself in 1881, but then went on to live a life as a performer and advocate for Native American rights, making him a popular figure both among whites and Native Americans.

Another famous Lakota leader was Red Cloud, from the Brule tribe. Red Cloud was able to convince several Native American tribes to band together to fight the U.S. Army in 1866, and led his people in several victories against them in what was later called Red Cloud's War. Because of his military prowess, the United States respected him as a serious opponent and eventually signed a peace treaty with him in 1868, allowing most of Red Cloud's demands. Red Cloud even visited Washington D.C. in 1870 to meet with President Ulysses S. Grant. Because of his contributions to his people and how respected he was by both friends and enemies, several major newspapers honored him after his death by printing recognitions of his achievements as both a leader and a diplomat.

Below are some examples from the passage of potential skimmed keywords and phrases that may help you understand the overall passage.

Sioux: (appears in the first sentence of many of the paragraphs and in the title of Figure 1)

Dakota: (appears in bold, in the italicized words *Eastern Dakota* and *Western Dakota*, as well as in Figure 1, and in the first sentence of several paragraphs)

Lakota: (appears in bold, in Figure 1, and in the first sentence of several paragraphs)

Classification: (is the premise of Figure 1 and appears in the title)

History: (appears in a heading)

The Dakota War of 1862: (appears in bold)

United States (U.S.): (appears in the first sentence of several paragraphs)

Famous figures: (appears in a heading)

<u>Red Cloud</u>: (appears inside of italicized words and the first sentence of the final paragraph)

After finding these words and checking just enough to see their meanings or how they are used in the passage, the reader should understand that the passage is about a group of Native Americans called the Sioux, who are divided into Lakota and Dakota groups. The reader should also be able to quickly know that this group must have been famous (they had famous figures such as Red Cloud) and fought with the United States (this keyword comes up frequently in the history section, along with the names of many wars). Use this information to answer the first comprehension question.

Comprehension Questions

1) What is this passage mainly about?
   (A) The history and classification of the Sioux
   (B) The classification of Native American tribes
   (C) Famous Lakota leaders
   (D) How Red Cloud was able to win his war

2) Which of the following is NOT true about Sitting Bull?
   (A) He was a member of the Hunkpapa tribe.
   (B) He helped defend his people from attacks by the United States.
   (C) He fought in the Dakota War of 1862.
   (D) He was popular because of his performances after surrendering.

3) What is the division between the Lakota and Dakota Sioux based on?
   (A) history
   (B) land area
   (C) culture
   (D) language

4) According to the passage, which year were the Sioux NOT involved in war?
   (A) 1720
   (B) 1805
   (C) 1866
   (D) 1876

5) In what year did Red Cloud meet the president of the United States?

    (A) 1866

    (B) 1868

    (C) 1870

    (D) 1890

Below are some examples of words that should be used for scanning in order to answer the questions.

Question 1: Skimming should be used; see the hints above the reading comprehension questions

Question 2: Sitting Bull, Hunkpapa, United States, Dakota War of 1862, perform, surrender

Question 3: Division, Lakota, Dakota

Question 4: War, battle, 1720, 1805, 1866, 1876

Question 5: Red Cloud, president, 1866, 1868, 1870, 1890

Explanation:

1. By skimming the article, you should know that the article discusses the classification of the Sioux, as well as their history (including famous people from their history). **A** is the only answer that includes references to both history and classification while also mentioning the specific group, the Sioux, so it is the best answer.

2. By scanning the passage, you should see that the article says "he was not involved in the initial conflicts, such as the Dakota War of 1862."

3. By skimming, you should realize that the information regarding classification (division) is discussed in the first paragraph. By scanning for *Dakota* and *Lakota*, you can quickly find that the text says this classification is based on language.

4. By scanning for the dates and checking for battles and wars during this time, you can quickly see that all of these years are marked by wars or battles, with the exception of 1805, which is the year the Sioux signed a treaty that brought peace to the area.

5. By skimming, you should realize that Red Cloud is discussed most in the last paragraph. By scanning for the word *president*, you should be able to quickly see that he met President Ulysses S. Grant in 1870.

See Page 121 for Answers

4. Paraphrasing and Summarizing

Paraphrasing is rewriting a statement in your own words, without necessarily shortening the original text. A well-written paraphrase should retain the main information of the original statement without changing the meaning or reusing the same words or phrases as the original.

Summarizing is rewriting passages to produce a condensed version of the original. A good summary should include all of the main ideas and major points of the original with relevant supporting evidence, while eliminating minor details.

> Paraphrasing and summarizing are necessary skills for writing academic papers and giving presentations. Paraphrasing and summarizing also demonstrate comprehension of the source material.

When writing paraphrases and summaries, use words and phrases that are different from the original source. If rewording is not possible, use direct quotations with proper referencing. Copying or presenting a source's exact words without citing the origin or author is **plagiarism**, which is a serious offense.

> To avoid committing plagiarism, learn how to summarize and paraphrase properly by mastering the techniques described below. However, be aware that paraphrasing still requires a citation that credits the original source.

Paraphrasing

The following steps can be used to create a paraphrase from an original passage:

Step 1: Change the parts of speech of some words in the original source by applying suffixes (see Chapter 1) or using other words in the same word family (see Chapter 2).

Original:	Students who love to read books are **generally** excited at **the prospect of** receiving scholarships.
Change 1:	**In general**, students who love to read books are excited by **prospective** scholarships.

<u>Step 2:</u> Consider changing the writing from passive to active voice or vice versa.

Change 1:   In general, **<u>students</u>** who love to read books **<u>are excited by</u>** prospective scholarships.

Change 2:   In general, prospective scholarships **<u>excite students</u>** who love to read books.

<u>Step 3:</u> Look for ways to utilize **reduction** – for example, changing a clause to a phrase. A **clause** is a group of words consisting of a subject and the finite form of a verb and might or might not be a sentence, whereas a **phrase** cannot stand alone as a sentence.

Change 2:   In general, prospective scholarships excite students **<u>who love to read books</u>**.

Change 3:   In general, prospective scholarships excite **<u>book-loving</u>** students.

The sentence is now structurally quite different from the original sentence.

<u>Step 4:</u> Replace some words in the original text with **synonyms** (see Chapter 2). Although proper nouns and specialized technical terms may not have synonyms, English has a rich variety of words with similar or identical meanings that can be used to avoid repeating too many words from an original sentence.

Change 3:   **<u>In general</u>**, prospective **<u>scholarships</u>** **<u>excite</u>** book-loving students.

Final: **<u>Typically</u>**, prospective **<u>financial aid</u>** **<u>thrills</u>** book-loving students.

Original: Students who love to read books are generally excited at the prospect of receiving scholarships.

Notice how different the final sentence is from the original. Sentences that are too similar to the original are not considered appropriate paraphrases. Be sure to use various combinations of the above techniques to ensure that your paraphrases are different enough from the original source. As a general rule, paraphrases and summaries should not include five or more words in a row directly taken from the original source.

Original	Albert Einstein is famous for his revolutionary theories of physics, which altered how we think about the universe.
Too similar	Albert Einstein's revolutionary theories of physics **<u>made him</u>** famous and altered how we think about the universe.
Too similar	Albert Einstein is famous for his **<u>novel</u>** theories of physics, which **<u>changed</u>** how we think about the universe.
Appropriate	**<u>Developing novel</u>** theories of physics that **<u>transformed</u>** our **<u>understanding of the</u>** universe **<u>made</u>** Albert Einstein **<u>world-renowned</u>**.

When trying to create an appropriate paraphrase, read the original sentence carefully and then re-write the important information from memory, without looking at the original.

Paraphrases do not necessarily need to have every piece of information as the original source but should include the main information and concepts. After writing a paraphrase, check that it does not change any of the important information in the original.

Language in Action:
Consider the following sentence and the following paraphrases.

Original	Birds migrate from areas of low or decreasing resources to areas of high or increasing resources, primarily for nesting and food resources.
Paraphrase 1	Birds migrate from places of low or decreasing resources to places of high or increasing resources, usually for nesting and food.
Paraphrase 2	When there is not enough food anymore, birds will fly from the north to the south.
Paraphrase 3	When faced with dwindling food or nesting resources, birds will often migrate to an area high or increasing in these resources.

Paraphrase 1 is too similar to the original sentence and is therefore not an appropriate paraphrase. **Paraphrase 2** is also inappropriate because it changes the meaning of the original passage too much; it does not mention nesting, and adds information about north and south, which was not in the original. **Paraphrase 3** is an appropriate paraphrase. Though it makes many changes to the original, it retains the important information (i.e., 1. *birds migrate due to a lack of food and nesting resources*, and 2. *birds migrate to high-resource areas*).

Summarizing

To summarize, first identify both the main idea of the text and the important supporting information. Next, write a shortened version of the original text that includes only these points and information. Summaries are often between 25 and 40% the length of the original passage, although this may vary depending on the purpose of your summary. Be sure to use tips from the paraphrasing section to avoid repeating too many words or phrases from the original, which may result in plagiarism.

1. Take Notes While Reading the Passage
Organize your notes by main points and supporting details (see Chapter 5).

2. Use the Notes to Write the Summary

When writing the summary, only use the notes. Do not look at the original text, as it will increase the chances of over-copying. Include only the main ideas and supporting evidence. Omit minor details, examples, and lengthy explanations.

3. Check the Summary

After summarizing, compare the summary with the original passage to ensure that:

1. It does not overuse words and phrases from the original text.
2. It is grammatically correct.
3. It is factually accurate with respect to the information in the original.

Comprehensive Example

Below is a reading passage followed by a short summary with paraphrases.

Original Article

Although there have been many tragic periods throughout European history, the Late Middle Ages is considered the most devastating. In fact, this era, typically defined as extending from 1250 to 1500, is often referred to as part of the Dark Ages. Its end ushered in a much brighter period for Europe, known as the Renaissance. While the Late Middle Ages saw many misfortunes, historians have identified the three most noteworthy calamities of the period as a devastating famine, a deadly plague, and an extended war.

Famines were common throughout much of the Late Middle Ages. However, a particularly prominent food shortage was the Great Famine of 1315–1317. In the spring of 1315, bad weather led to massive crop failures. To make matters worse, the crop failures coincided with a number of animal diseases that killed 80% of the livestock used for food. The resulting famine lasted for over two years. During that time, it is estimated that between 10% and 20% of people living in urban areas starved to death. Those that remained were forced to turn to begging, crime, and even cannibalism to survive.

However, an even darker period in European history came about 30 years later, when the continent was overcome with the bubonic plague, also known as the Black Death. Over a four-year period, this lethal pandemic caused somewhere between 25 and 200 million deaths. In addition, the pestilence affected the economies of Europe in profound ways by shrinking the labor force, increasing wages, and causing unprecedented morbidity among the peasant class.

The longest military conflict in European history also occurred during the Late Middle Ages. Although it is known as the Hundred Years' War, the conflict actually lasted 116 years, from 1337 to 1453, and took the lives of two to three million people. The entire war actually consisted of three Anglo-Franco conflicts lasting 23 years, 20 years, and 38 years, respectively. The hostilities were punctuated by two truces, one lasting nine years and the other 26. The cause of the war was the gradual buildup of tensions regarding which branch of the various French and English monarchies should take control of the male line of the Capetian dynasty and thereby assume the French throne. In the end, the House of Valois – one of the French monarchies – was victorious.

Summary with Paraphrases

Three significant deadly catastrophes occurred in Europe during the Late Middle Ages (1250–1500): widespread starvation, a lethal epidemic, and unrelenting fighting. Mass starvation was caused by bad weather, which led to agricultural failures and lethal cattle diseases from 1315 to 1317. This killed much of the population and drove others to begging, crime, and even cannibalism. The most notable epidemic was the Black Death, which peaked between 1347 and 1351 and killed between 25 and 200 million people, while also severely affecting the economies of Europe. Lastly, the predominant war of the period was the so-called Hundred Years' War, which was actually three conflicts that raged between 1337 and 1453. The war began as a result of the long-standing animosity between the various royal houses of France and England regarding the male lineage of the Capetian dynasty, which held the rights to the French throne.

<u>English I-B</u>

Academic Listening and Speaking

Objective 1: Take and discuss notes

5. Note-Taking While Listening
6. Orally Summarizing from Notes

Objective 2: Use common spoken academic expressions

7. Idiomatic Language
8. Interrogatives and Stating Opinions

5. Note-Taking While Listening

Note-taking is essential in academic settings. Organizing information can help you to remember important information. Taking notes is also key to comprehension when listening to academic lectures. Writing down what a speaker says also helps listeners be more attentive. It makes the listener responsible for identifying **key information** and **organizing** the information clearly.

> Learning to listen for gist and taking well-organized notes will help you when attending lectures and participating in laboratory activities. When listening to lectures and explanations, you will need to remember or study the information later, but only have one opportunity to hear it.

Listening to a lecture, speech, or lengthy conversation is different from actively *participating* in a discussion. Lectures, speeches, presentations, and talks are usually structured, and sometimes written or scripted by the speaker ahead of time. Academic lectures usually contain specific, important information, called **key information**, that may be included later on an exam, or required for writing essays or reports.

> While there are several different ways to take notes, all styles require the note-taker to listen for **signal words and phrases**, **organize** the notes logically, and write down **facts** and **key words** quickly.

Identifying Information via Key Words and Phrases

Signal words and phrases help listeners to identify **main ideas** and **supporting details** and understand how the information is connected. Context clues can also help you to distinguish between main ideas and supporting details.

> When a speaker gives a lecture or long talk in English, they will use signal words and phrases, as well as repetition, and tone of voice (see Chapter 14) to give the listener clues about important information.

Carefully read over the common signal words and phrases in Tables 1 and 2. Identify those you already know and focus on learning new signal words or phrases. These chunks of language are often called **sentence starters**. Most speakers will vary how they use these phrases. Make sure to listen to the information that follows these signal words and phrases. The words in parentheses are not necessary, but often occur together with the other words.

> Note that what you hear is not exactly what would be written. For example, you will often hear fluent speakers of English say, "I'm gonna…" while they write, "I'm going to…" In an academic lecture, an expert or professor is less likely to use contracted phrases such as *gonna*, *wanna* (want to), or *shoulda* (should have), but during fast speech, these informal contractions are often unavoidable.

Table 1. Signal Words and Phrases for Introducing Topics and Changing Main Ideas

Introducing Topics			
Today…	(What) We are / were discussing is…	I'm going to / I want to talk about…	What is…?
Introducing or Changing Main Ideas			
Let's look at…	First, second, third…/ another / the next (point)	Let's move on…	Important / main / major / critical / key
I'd like to mention…	You should note (that)…	The role of…	

Table 2. Signal Words and Phrases for Introducing Details about Topics and Main Ideas

Giving Facts and Numbers			
You might want to know / ought to know (that)…	As you can see…	Keep in mind (that)…	The relationship/ difference between…
In the sense that…	Well…	In fact…	Basically…
Giving Explanations			
(so) You can see (that) … (from)…	You see…	The thing is…	(See) What I'm saying is…
If you think about it…	In other words…	In this respect…	But first…/ however / though
Giving Reasons and Results			
It turns out (that)…	In order to…	The reason why / for…	In turn…
…leads to…	Because…	Therefore…	

Giving Examples			
Take <example>	If you look at…	When you look at…	Including / like /…and so forth
For example / an example of…	For instance…		
Defining Terms			
…referred to as…	…which is (called)…	…(also) known as…	According to…

Organizing Information

In note-taking, it is important to show how different pieces of information relate to one another. The information is broadly classified into two categories: main ideas and supporting details. These categories can be further divided, as shown in Tables 1 and 2.

Use these guidelines to help you organize your notes as you write:
1. Write each main idea you hear on a single line.
2. Write all of the related supporting details for each main idea underneath the appropriate main idea.

A speaker will probably only have one general topic, but will usually have several main points. Consider writing one or two broad terms for the topic at the top of the page.

Well organized notes might look like the following:

```
                        TOPIC
   1.  First main idea
          → Facts and numbers
          → Explanations
          → Reasons and results
          → Examples
          → Term definitions
   2.  Second main idea
```

The supporting details in lectures and long talks are the same as those given in writing, as discussed in Chapter 12. However, some words and phrases are more common in spoken English than written English (compare the tables in this chapter and those in Chapter 12).

Writing Quickly

Whether in a course of study at a university or doing research, taking notes about a written text does not require speed. However, when listening to a lecture or presentation, it is nearly impossible for listeners to write at the same pace as the person is speaking. Typically, the lecturer or speaker will continue to talk, so you have to write quickly so that you can continue to pay attention in order to grasp new information.

Here are some tips for writing quickly and efficiently when taking notes:

1. Use abbreviations and symbols

Abbreviations are shortened forms of words, and **symbols** are used in place of words. Abbreviations and symbols may be standardized or personal.

- Some abbreviations (e.g., *World Health Organization → WHO, United States of America → USA*) are standardized because they are well-known.

- You can also use personalized abbreviations, as long as you can easily identify them later (e.g., *international → int'l, government → gov't*)

- There are some well-known symbols for some words (e.g., *and → &*), but there may be other alternatives (e.g., *and → +*)

- Use the abbreviations and symbols that are the easiest for _you_ to write and recognize.

Below are some common abbreviations and symbols to consider using.

with, without	w/, w/o	**about/regarding**	re:
because	b/c	**number**	#, No.
chapter	ch.	**and**	&, +
for example	e.g.	**is / equals**	=
specifically	i.e.	**at**	@
definition	def.	**increase / decrease**	↑ / ↓

2. Write phrases, not full sentences

When taking notes during a lecture, there will probably not be enough time to write full sentences. Consider reducing important information to simple phrases.

Instead of writing a long sentence such as:

World War II took place between 1939 and 1945 among America, Britain, France, Soviets, Germany, Italy, and Japan.

Shorten the information into a note such as:

WWII: 1939–1945 among US, GB, FR, USSR, DE, IT, JPN.

3. Paraphrase

To paraphrase is to re-write a speaker or writer's words in your own words. The main aim of paraphrasing during note-taking while listening is to produce a shortened version of a speech or lecture. You do not need to write exactly what the speaker said. Chapter 4 provides more details about paraphrasing in writing.

> Aim to correctly represent the main ideas and the important supporting details. Remove any unnecessary words from the speaker's remarks and write in a way that is true to the lecture or talk, but is short and easy to understand.

Instead of writing the speaker's exact words, such as:

So anyway, it is important to know that Vincent van Gogh was never a commercially successful painter because his work didn't sell well until after his death.

Shorten by paraphrasing, such as:

van Gogh didn't make money painting; his art sold better after he died.

Other Tips for Note-Taking While Listening

Prepare for academic lectures or talks.

- Do any *assigned reading or research* before the lecture.
- For standardized tests, *look over the questions* before listening in order to guess what information to pay attention to.
- If a professor or speaker distributes handouts before a lecture, try to *anticipate* or *make predictions* about what will be said based on what is written in them.
- Leave *blank space* when taking notes. You might miss important information while listening to a lecture. You can write the information that you missed later in the blank space.

> Don't be afraid to ask questions of the speaker, classmates, or others who can provide you with information that you might have missed.

<u>Comprehensive Example</u>

 Listen to the audio file on the Pathways Website!

Listen to the lecture. Look at the transcript below and the sample notes about this topic and notice the following:

1. The signal words and phrases, highlighted in **bold**, clearly mark the important information (underlined).
2. The notes are well organized. It is clear what the main points are and which supporting details are attached to which main points.
3. The notes make good use of abbreviations, symbols, phrases, and paraphrasing.

Example lecture transcript

> Okay, um, so **today we are going to talk about** what plants do for the ecosystem, which is academically **referred to as** "ecological services." These services are how plants support other members of the ecosystem, specifically animals. In this lesson, I'm going to outline how several of these "ecological services" work. **The first** of these key services is **known as** the carbon-oxygen cycle. The basis of this cycle is photosynthesis, **which is** when a plant absorbs carbon dioxide from the atmosphere and water from the ground to produce oxygen and glucose for plant growth. We talked about this a little bit last class, but I, I really want to mention here that this process is so important because when animals breathe, they convert oxygen into carbon dioxide, so **in fact**, they need plants to create oxygen for their survival. So, remember to thank a plant for your oxygen today. Furthermore, when plants die, they decompose, and the carbon returns to the soil so that it can be utilized by other plants and animals. Now, let's uh…, **let's move on** to **talk about** how plants also provide energy for the entire ecosystem. **Keep in mind that** plants get the energy needed for photosynthesis directly from the sun. If you, um, if you did your homework, you should know that already. **If you think about it**, animals cannot create energy themselves, so they have to eat these plants or other animals for energy. Maybe you think that carnivores don't need plants, but **the thing is**, even if an animal does not eat plants directly, it eats animals that do, so **in other words**, all animals rely on plants for energy…

Example of notes based on the above lecture

Ecological services
→ what plants do for the ecosystem
→ support ecosystem members (i.e. animals)

1. Carbon-oxygen cycle
→ photosynthesis = absorb CO_2 & water → oxygen & glucose
→ animals need plants b/c their breathing = oxygen → CO_2
→ plant death = carbon returns to soil for others' use

2. Provide Energy
→ plants get energy from sun
→ animals cannot get energy from sun
→ animals rely on plants b/c they eat plants or other animals

---

6. Orally Summarizing from Notes

Students in English language learning environments are often expected to be able to give oral summaries of a lecture, talk, reading, or recording. Giving an oral summary from notes consists of determining important information and verbally communicating it.

> You must become able to discuss your notes in order to check their accuracy. The first step is to orally summarize your notes.

The following three basic steps can help you present a successful oral summary of your notes:
1. Identify the main ideas and important supporting details
2. Organize the information clearly
3. Verbally communicate the relevant information

Identifying the Important Information

All of the main ideas from the source material (lecture, talk, reading, etc.) must be included in an oral summary. Also, most of the important supporting details (i.e., facts, explanations, reasons, examples, and definitions) should also be included.

> If you take well-organized notes while listening to a lecture (see Chapter 5), you can use the notes to identify key information. Also, be sure to use your own words. An oral summary consists of paraphrasing spoken or written content, not just repeating exactly what has been heard or read.

Organizing the Information Clearly

Creating a basic outline of your notes can make it easier to produce a summary. The outline does not need to be too detailed. It should simply serve as a reference for the logical order of what is stated. The outline of information helps you orally summarize by introducing the main ideas of the topic, elaborating on the details, and using transition vocabulary to switch between main ideas.

Here is an example of an outline organized in the topic – main points – supporting information format:

I. TOPIC: *Sea mammals*

II. MAIN POINT:
Similarity with land mammals

III. SUPPORTING INFORMATION
    A. ***Oxygen intake***
        1. *Surface breathing*
            a. *Manatees*
    B. ***Nourishing young***
        1. *Milk*
            a. *Dolphins*
    C. ***Hair follicles***
        1. *Hair-like structures*
            a. *Sea otters*

Verbally Communicating the Information

Although pronunciation and intonation (see Chapter 15) are important when speaking, the most important skill for orally summarizing notes is the clear communication of ideas. To effectively communicate your notes orally, learn the phrases in Table 1, and beware of common mistakes.

Table 1. Phrases Useful for Orally Summarizing Notes

Introducing a Main Point	Elaborating on Points	Transitioning
The first (second/third) point brought up by the speaker/author is…	One (another) reason the speaker/author thinks so is that…	This brings up another major point/reason/issue…
The main reason for this is…	One (another) example that shows this is…	Moving on to the next (second/third) point/issue…
One (another) important issue the speaker/author talks about is…	Also/furthermore/in addition, the speaker/author mentions that…	However, the speaker/author also has another important issue/point…
One (another) major topic is…	Specifically, the speaker/author says that…	For example, the speaker/author points out that…

When orally summarizing your notes, you can also use the **signal words and phrases** from Chapter 5, as well as other useful phrases and words found in other chapters.

When orally summarizing your notes, use complete sentences and proper transition vocabulary. Avoid the following common mistakes so that you do not confuse listeners:

1. Do not leave out the sentence's subject or premise (main idea).
2. Be aware that overuse of the word *so* can accidentally create a logical connection between two sentences that does not exist.

Examples of these mistakes and how to correct them are shown in Table 2.

Table 2. Common Mistakes Made When Orally Summarizing Notes

	Mistake	**Corrected**
Missing subject or premise	Talks about climate change.	→ The passage talks about climate change.
	Changes in DNA by virus.	→ Viruses cause changes in DNA.
Unrelated information or improperly connected information	Many people are worried… so global warming is getting serious.	→ Many people are worried because global warming is getting serious.
	Virus DNA changes… so scientists study the DNA of some plants.	→ Studying the DNA of some plants helps scientists understand how virus DNA can change.
	Recycling is important… so it is damaging the Earth.	→ Recycling is important… because not doing it is damaging the Earth.

Comprehensive Example

 Listen to the audio file on the Pathways Website!

Look at the sample notes from Chapter 5. Below is an example of an outline of an oral summary of these notes. Listen to the oral summary by downloading the audio file from www.pathwaysto academicenglish.com. Read the transcript of the oral summary while listening and notice that:

1. The summary is shorter than the original lecture in Chapter 5, but uses some of the key vocabulary (i.e., *ecosystem, ecological, photosynthesis*).
2. The sentences are simpler, have clear subjects, and use the words and phrases introduced in this chapter, highlighted in **bold**.

Outline for Oral Summary

```
I. TOPIC:
What plants do for the ecosystem: Ecological services


II. MAIN POINT 1:
Carbon-oxygen cycle


III. SUPPORTING INFORMATION
 A. Photosynthesis
  1. Absorb CO₂ & water
  2. Makes oxygen & glucose
 B. Animals need plants
  1. They breathe oxygen
  2. Make CO₂
 C. Plant death
  1. Gives carbon back to soil for others


IV. MAIN POINT 2:
Provide Energy


V. SUPPORTING INFORMATION
 A. Plants get energy from the sun
  1. Through photosynthesis
  2. Animals cannot
 B. Animals need plants
  1. They have to eat plants or animals for energy
```

Example Oral Summary

The **speaker talked about** how plants support the ecosystem through "ecological services." The **first point he introduced** was one of these services, **specifically** the carbon-oxygen cycle. **The key feature of** this cycle is photosynthesis. **The speaker mentioned** that plants use carbon dioxide and water to turn it into oxygen and glucose. **In addition, he mentioned** that animals need plants to do this because they breathe oxygen and make carbon dioxide. **He also pointed out** that when plants die, they give carbon back to the soil so that others can use it. **Moving on, the other ecological service is** providing energy. **The speaker says that** plants get energy from the sun through photosynthesis, and that animals cannot. **Specifically, he says that** animals need plants for their energy because they have to eat plants or other animals for energy instead.

7. Idiomatic Language

Idiomatic language consists of words or phrases that are not interpreted according to their literal or dictionary meaning. This chapter will introduce four types of idiomatic language:

1. Metaphors
2. Phrasal verbs
3. Idiomatic expressions
4. Idioms

Even though idiomatic language is not used extensively in written English, it is important to understand it because it is extremely common in spoken English – in everyday conversations, academic presentations, lectures, and classroom discussions. Becoming more familiar with how idiomatic language is used, in what situations it is used, and how to interpret it will greatly improve your listening and speaking skills.

> You can begin to master idiomatic language by paying attention to patterns and concepts. This can improve your ability to guess the actual meaning of idiomatic language in context, even if the expression is unfamiliar to you.

Metaphors

Metaphors are expressions that are used to make a comparison between two things that are not completely alike but may have something in common. Look at the following sentences:

> Life is a rollercoaster ride.
> She cried a river of tears.

The meanings of these sentences are not literal, but the essence is understood. Life is not actually a ride on a rollercoaster, but both things have ups and downs. Rivers are not made of tears, but both tears and rivers consist of flowing liquids.

Metaphors are usually based on **cultural concepts**. People who share cultural concepts can make metaphorical comparisons easily and naturally. Understanding these concepts (even if you do not agree with them) can help you guess the meanings of English metaphors.

Table 1. Common Cultural Concepts and Metaphors in English

	Cultural Concept	**Metaphor Example**	**Meaning of Example**
1	**upward** as *positive*	She's <u>flying high</u> in her new job.	She is doing very well in her new job.
2	**downward** as *negative*	He's been <u>down in the dumps</u> all day.	He's been depressed all day.
3	**time** as *money*	His mistake <u>cost</u> us 10 hours.	His mistake wasted 10 hours.
4	**hardness** as *strength*	She is my <u>rock</u>.	I rely on her for her strength.
5	**argument** as *war*	He <u>shot</u> my thesis <u>full of holes</u>.	He said my thesis was not valid.
6	**sports** as *war*	Our <u>team was killed</u> yesterday!	Our team lost yesterday.
7	**life** as *a journey*	Our relationship is <u>at a crossroads</u>.	We must decide how our relationship will continue.
8	**ideas** as *items for sale*	I'm not <u>buying</u> your story.	I don't believe your story.
9	**effort** as *plants*	All of our hard work has finally <u>borne fruit</u>.	Our hard work has finally led to good results.
10	**things** as *people* (personification)	<u>Opportunity</u> was knocking at my door.	I received an opportunity.
11	**overstated descriptions** (exaggeration)	<u>A million people</u> came to my house last night.	Many people came to my house last night.

Phrasal Verbs

Phrasal verbs consist of a verb and a **particle or preposition** like *in*, *on*, *off*, or *out*, that together create a meaning different from that of the original verb.

The verb **catch** can mean *to grasp something with one's hands*, and the preposition **on** means *physically in contact with something*. When these two words combine to form the phrasal verb **catch on**, the meaning changes to *to come into contact with something and grasp it*. It can also have other meanings, such as *to become popular* or *to become aware of something*.

Phrasal verbs often have more than one meaning because prepositions may have up to four different meanings:

- a location meaning
- a motion meaning
- a change meaning
- another uncategorized meaning

English language learners are usually familiar with the most common meaning of prepositions – locations (in time or space) – but are often not familiar with the other three types of meanings.

The four types of preposition meanings are often connected idiomatically. By learning the most common meanings and understanding the relationships between verbs and prepositions in phrasal verbs, students can begin to guess the meanings of unfamiliar phrasal verbs in context.

Look at the common preposition meanings in Table 2 and read the explanations for guessing the meaning of phrasal verbs using this knowledge.

Table 2. Common Meanings of Prepositions in Phrasal Verbs

	Preposition	Motion Meaning	Change Meaning	Other Meaning
1	across	to move from one side of something to the other		
2	after	to follow or chase		
3	along	to move on a set path or the same path as something else		to do something at the same time or together
4	apart		to change from being whole to being in pieces	
5	around, about	to move in a circle, to move in various places near something		
6	away (from)	to move to a more distant position	to disappear	
7	back	to move to the original position or backwards	to return to the original state	
8	down	to move from a higher position to a lower one	to become less, worse, lower, degraded	to finish, realize, achieve or attain
9	in, into	to enter		
10	off (of)	to move to a position of not touching	to become unattached	
11	on, onto	to move to a position of touching	to become attached	to continue
12	out (of)	to exit	to disappear, to appear	to do completely (causing something to be eliminated)

	Preposition	Motion Meaning	Change Meaning	Other Meaning
13	over	to move to a higher position than something else or traverse it	to reverse; to change from a standing position to another position	
14	through	to move into something from one side and then exit it from the other		
15	together		to change from being in pieces to being whole	
16	under, below	to move to a lower position than something else		
17	up	to move from a lower position to a higher one	to become more, better, higher, improved	to do completely, properly, or well

Guessing the Meanings of Phrasal Verbs

To guess which meaning a preposition might take in a phrasal verb, consider the verb type. If the verb is _be_, the preposition will usually take on the **location meaning**. For instance, _be in_ means _to be inside of something_, such as in "_The book **is in** the bag._"

If a **verb of movement** is used, like _run_, _fly_, or _walk_, the preposition will take on the **motion meaning** and indicate the **direction** of the motion. Look at Table 2 and notice that _in_ can mean _to enter_. Therefore:

- _**run in**_ means _enter by running_
- _**jump in**_ means _enter by jumping_
- _**fly in**_ means _enter by flying_

Some verbs describe an **action or change**, such as _fade_ or _cut_. When combined with these types of verbs, the preposition will generally take on the **change meaning** and indicate the **final result** of the change. Look at Table 2 and notice that _away_ can mean _to disappear_. Therefore:

- _**fade away**_ means _disappear slowly from view_
- _**burn away**_ means _disappear in fire or smoke_
- _**wash away**_ means _make disappear by the act of washing or the flow of water_

Table 3 contains some of the common types of verbs with meanings that indicate location, motion, or change.

Table 3. Common Verbs Found in Various Types of Phrasal Verbs

common verbs of state or location	*be, exist, sit, lay*
common verbs of movement	1. **simple verbs:** *go, come, get* 2. **verbs of motion:** *run, walk, roll, fly, jump* 3. **verbs of transportation:** *drive, fly, ride*
common verbs of action or change	1. **simple verbs:** *get, take, pick, turn, go, come*, fall** 2. **action verbs:** *push, pull, put, set, kick, cut, flip, work* 3. **tools or instruments as verbs:** *glue, staple, tape, saw* 4. **onomatopoeia:** *click, knock, bump, smash, crack*

common verbs that take uncategorized meanings	**up**	• goes with **most verbs** • verb with **positive** connotations (e.g., *clean, cheer, dress*)
	down	• verbs with **negative** connotations (e.g., *close, break*) • verbs with **clear goals** (e.g., *chase, hunt*)
	out	• verbs indicating a **problem or mystery** is being eliminated (e.g., *figure out, find out, work out*) • verbs indicating a **chance** is being eliminated (e.g., *miss out, strike out*) • verbs indicating **items/stock** is being eliminated (e.g., *run out, sell out*)

*When "come" and "fall" are used as change verbs, they usually indicate that the change happened on its own, and was not caused by an outside force or action.

Understanding how prepositions and verbs can combine to create new meanings can help you to guess the meanings of many phrasal verbs in context.

> Some of the common phrasal verbs in Table 4 have meanings that cannot be guessed based on the information above. You will have to learn these extra meanings over time.

Some phrasal verbs have meanings that are not easily guessed, so it helps to look for **context clues**. For example, *work out* can mean *to solve a problem through effort* or *to exercise*. Look at the sentences below and notice how the surrounding words give you clues as to which meaning *work out* takes in each sentence.

My professor helped me to **work out** the problems in my experiment. (=*solve a problem*)

I gained too much weight, so I started to **work out** three times a week. (*=exercise*)

Table 4. Common Phrasal Verbs Found in Academic English

1. *look* **after**	9. *carry* **on**	17. *find* **out**	25. *take* **over**
2. *go* **away**	10. *come* **on**	18. *get* **out**	26. *go* **through**
3. *come* **back**	11. *get* **on/off**	19. *go* **out**	27. *end* **up**
4. *get* **back**	12. *go* **on**	20. *point* **out**	28. *follow* **up**
5. *go* **back**	13. *take* **on**	21. *set* **out**	29. *get* **up**
6. *get* **in**	14. *work* **on**	22. *sort* **out**	30. *pick* **up**
7. *go* **in**	15. *carry* **out**	23. *turn* **out**	31. *set* **up**
8. *go* **off**	16. *come* **out**	24. *work* **out**	32. *take* **up**

Idiomatic Expressions

The meanings of **idiomatic expressions** cannot be easily guessed using any particular techniques. They are best learned in context, whether spoken or written. Table 5 contains the 37 most common idiomatic expressions used in academic English.

> Some phrases contain the gender-neutral indefinite pronoun *one*, meaning a person. These are not usually used in writing or speaking, but serve as a model. When using these idioms or idiomatic expressions, be sure to replace *one* with the appropriate specific pronoun. For example, *slip one's mind* means *to forget*, so it should be changed as follows:
>
> It slipped *my* mind. (= I forgot.)
> It slipped *his* mind. (= He forgot.)
>
> Notice how these expressions are used by checking example sentences. For example, *slip one's mind* is usually used in the past tense to downplay forgetting something.

Table 5. List of most Common Idiomatic Expressions in Academic English

	Phrase	Meaning	Example Sentence
	Time Related		
1	at some point	occurring at some time that is not yet definite	I want you to check my paper **at some point**. When are you free?
2	at the moment	right now	I'm busy **at the moment**. Please come back later.

	Phrase	Meaning	Example Sentence
3	at the time	occurring at the time being discussed	I didn't know you were a student **at the time**. I thought you had graduated by then.
4	put time into	make effort, spend time doing	I **put a lot of time into** my project, so I got a good grade.
5	so far	up to the current point in time; to a limited extent	1. **So far**, this is his best novel. 2. Studying English will only take you **so far**. You'll have to actually use it to get better.
Opinions			
6	beats me	to not know	A: What time does the meeting start? B: **Beats me**.
7	benefit of the doubt	to use a judgement despite uncertainty	I don't know if he was really sick or not, but I will give him the **benefit of the doubt**.
8	go for	to want	I could **go for** a break. I've been studying for four hours straight!
9	no doubt	it is certain	There is **no doubt** that the earth is round.
10	point of view	one's opinion or feelings	His **point of view** is different from the rest of the team's.
11	see what one is saying	to understand someone's opinion or idea	I **see what you are saying**, but I disagree.
12	shake one's head	to disagree or refuse	I asked if she would help, but she just **shook her head**.
13	slip one's mind	to forget	I didn't go to the meeting because it **slipped my mind**.
Cause and Effect			
14	bound to	will probably happen	With all the studying you have been doing, you are **bound to** pass the test.
15	in the event (of/that)	if something happens	**In the event of** rain, the game will be cancelled.
16	lead to	to cause	Eating less and exercising more **leads to** weight loss.
Work and Effort			
17	cut someone some slack	to allow more freedom or be more forgiving than usual	Because he was sick, his teacher **cut him some slack** with the assignment deadline.

	Phrase	Meaning	Example Sentence
18	deal with	to take action, manage, handle, or treat	Only team leaders should **deal with** the administration office.
19	find oneself doing something	to do something naturally, without conscious intention	At her new job, she **found herself applying the skills** she had learned in university.
20	for the sake of	the purpose or reason, in consideration of	1. My essay was not easy to understand, so I rewrote it **for the sake of** clarity. 2. **For the sake of** other people's health, we should wear face masks when sick.
21	no matter what it takes	to do anything necessary to achieve something	We will work all night if we have to, because we have to finish the report, **no matter what it takes!**
22	take advantage of	to make good use of an opportunity; to exploit	1. We should **take advantage of** the library while it is still open. 2. He **took advantage of** my weakness.
23	take for granted	to fail to properly appreciate; to assume that something is true	1. I **took** my parent's generosity **for granted**. 2. I **took** it **for granted** that I would be paid for my work.
Interpersonal Feelings			
24	add insult to injury	to make a bad situation even worse	My boss not only said I could not get a pay increase in future, but **to add insult to injury,** he reduced my current pay.
25	be in someone's shoes	to be in the same situation as someone else	If I **were in your shoe**s, I wouldn't drive in heavy rain at night.
26	hang in there	to not give up	Maya didn't want to keep studying, but she **hung in there** and finally finished.
27	hit it off	to form a good relationship with someone quickly	Luckily, I really **hit it off** with my new lab mate.
28	in touch with	to contact	Please keep **in touch with** your parents or else they will worry.
29	on one's own	to receive no help	He asked for help with his paper, but I am busy, so he's **on his own**.
30	pull oneself together	to recover self-control and be calm	Bob was shocked after the car accident, but after he **pulled himself together**, he called the police.

	Phrase	Meaning	Example Sentence
31	read between the lines	to find meaning that is not clearly stated, only implied	He said we had done enough, but **reading between the lines**, I knew that he thought we should have done more.
32	take it easy	to relax, to work at a comfortable pace	A: I have so much to do today! B: Well, **take it easy**!
Amounts or Comparisons			
33	a good/great deal of	many/much	Students at Tohoku University spend **a good deal of** their time in the library.
34	as opposed to	in contrast to	Students here learn two foreign languages **as opposed to** other universities where they only learn English.
35	by all means	absolutely	A: May I have a look at your lab report? B: **By all means**.
36	by no means	absolutely not	Even though some people come to class late, it is **by no means** acceptable to do so.
37	something like	approximately	**Something like** 500 people showed up to the festival.

Idioms

Idioms are similar to the idiomatic expressions above, but tend to have historical, cultural, literary, or proverbial origins. Table 6 is a list of common English idioms that are heard in everyday speech and often appear in high-interest texts.

Table 6. List of most Common Idioms in English

	Idiom	Meaning	Example Sentence
1	a far cry from	very different	The weather in Hawaii is **a far cry from** the weather in Hokkaido.
2	cost an arm and a leg	very expensive	The airfare to Europe **costs an arm and a leg** these days.
3	call it a day	to stop working on something	We've done enough work. Let's **call it a day**.
4	fall into one's lap	to get something by luck or coincidence without effort	Good grades seem to **fall into her lap** for every class.

	Idiom	Meaning	Example Sentence
5	get cold feet	to suddenly have the feeling of not wanting to do something that was planned	She's **getting cold feet** about her wedding tomorrow.
6	head over heels	to be in love, especially in the beginning of a relationship	He has been **head over heels** for her ever since they met.
7	hit the nail on the head	to do or say something perfectly	You really **hit the nail on the head** with your answer today.
8	hit the sack/hay	go to sleep	I'm going to **hit the sack** around midnight.
9	let the cat out of the bag	to tell or reveal a secret	Please don't **let the cat out of the bag** about me moving to Tokyo.
10	like the back of one's hand	to know something very well	I know Shinjuku **like the back of my hand.**
11	on the ball	to be attentive, and quick to act	Our new employee is really **on the ball.**
12	on the fence	to be indecisive	He's **on the fence** about attending a public or private university.
13	once in a blue moon	very rarely	I swim in the ocean **once in a blue moon.**
14	over one's head	too difficult to do	Those mathematical equations are easy for us but they are **over the heads of our students.**
15	piece of cake	very easy	That test was a **piece of cake.**
16	play by ear	to do something without a plan	I'm going to **play** this weekend **by ear.**
17	take the bull by the horns	to deal with a difficult situation in a very direct way	In this job, you'll have to **take the bull by the horns.**
18	take with a grain of salt	to not take something you are told seriously, because it may be untrue	I usually **take** the news that I read on Facebook **with a grain of salt.**
19	the last straw	the last in a series of small bad things to happen that finally causes one big bad thing to happen	I forgave his poor work because he was new, but being late today **was the last straw.** I'm going to have to fire him.
20	under the weather	feeling ill	I'm **under the weather**, so I won't be coming in to work today.

Comprehensive Example

 Listen to the audio file on the Pathways Website!

Look at the example conversations below and notice the examples of various types of idiomatic language (in **bold**). Listen to the conversations by downloading the audio file from www.pathwaystoacademicenglish.com and then answer the questions.

Example Conversation 1

MAN: Oh no! I spilled coffee on my white shirt! Is there any way I can get this stain to **come out**?

WOMAN: I'm not sure, but I don't think just putting it into the washing machine will clean it. You'll probably have to **steam it out.**

MAN: Steam it out? That's **over my head**.

WOMAN: Mine too. You'd better leave it to professionals. Do you want me to **drop it off** at the dry-cleaning shop for you?

---

1) What does the phrasal verb "come out" mean in this situation?
   (A) go back to what it was before
   (B) come to the dry-cleaning shop
   (C) be removed
   (D) have coffee

2) How does the woman suggest the man clean the shirt?
   (A) by steaming it
   (B) by all means
   (C) with coffee
   (D) by washing it

3) What does the woman offer to do?
   (A) have coffee with the man
   (B) clean the man's shirt
   (C) put the shirt over the man's head
   (D) take the shirt to the dry-cleaning shop

Example Conversation 2

MAN: What do you think about this advertisement for a part-time job selling insurance policies? I could **go for** some extra money.

WOMAN: I think applying would be a **waste of time**. You're always **searching for easy ways to make money**, but you should focus on something more stable. This job doesn't pay an hourly wage. It's all commission – you'll only get paid if you sell a lot of policies.

MAN: I know, but it says there will be opportunities for the position to **branch out** in the future.

WOMAN: Perhaps. But I think this company will **take advantage of** you at the beginning. You may **find yourself working** hard for no pay.

MAN: Well, I think that I'll give them **the benefit of the doubt**.

WOMAN: OK. Why don't you try it out for a month or so? If you don't see **the fruits of your labor** by then you should quit.

---

4) What does the woman think will happen if the man gets the job?

(A) He will get the benefit of the doubt.

(B) He will search for an easier job.

(C) He won't make any money.

(D) He will work at a fruit farm.

5) What is the man likely to do?

(A) Discuss the advantages and disadvantages of the job

(B) Quit the job after a month

(C) Branch out in the future

(D) Apply for the job

See Page 121 for Answers

8. Interrogatives and Stating Opinions

An **interrogative** is a word or sentence used to ask a question. Forming grammatically correct questions is a fundamental skill in English that students will need when requesting information. When answering questions, you will often be required to give your opinion and defend your position with facts, details, and evidence.

> Mastering the ability to form questions is an essential skill for participating in a wide variety of academic activities such as group work, discussions, and research.

The following are required to improve your ability to form interrogatives and state your opinion convincingly:

1. Review the word order, meanings, and proper responses to basic questions.
2. Be aware of the functions of special interrogatives such as rhetorical and embedded questions.
3. Know how to respond to special interrogatives and common greetings.
4. Learn several ways to state and support opinions with facts, details, and evidence.

Common Mistakes with Interrogatives

Review the word order, meanings, and responses to basic questions by checking the **common mistakes** made by Japanese learners of English below.

1. Confusing direct and open-ended questions

Direct questions (or closed questions) can be answered simply with *yes* or *no*.

Open-ended questions require a constructed response.

> **Direct:** Are you a university student? → Yes.
> **Open-ended:** What university do you attend? → ~~Yes.~~ I attend Tohoku University.

2. Not moving nouns modified by wh-question word determiners to the head of a sentence

When *wh*-**question words** are used as determiners (*what, which whose*), the noun that is being clarified must be placed directly after the *wh*-question word.

> ~~What do you like sports?~~ What sport do you like?
> ~~Which shall we eat first sushi?~~ Which sushi shall we eat first?

3. Confusing wh-question words used as adverbs

Wh-question words used as adverbs refer to times, locations, methods, purposes, or reasons. Some have specific purposes, such as ***how old*** for **ages**, ***how far*** for **distances** and ***how come*** for **reasons** or **explanations**.

> ~~How many years is that house?~~ **How old** is that house?
> ~~How much distance is it to your house?~~ **How far** is it to your house?
> ~~How are you studying?~~ **How come** you're studying? → Because I have a test.
> (*how come* is the same as *why*)

4. Incorrectly answering negative questions

When answering **negative questions**, including **tag questions**, the positive equivalent of the question (without implication) and not the actual question itself should be answered.

- Answers that begin with *yes* should never be followed by negative statements.
- Answers that begin with *no* should never be followed by positive statements.

> Didn't you enjoy Dr. Smith's lecture? → ~~Yes, I didn't.~~ **No**, I didn't (enjoy the lecture).
> You don't like pizza, do you? ~~No, I do.~~ **Yes**, I do (like pizza).

Interrogatives as Common Greetings

Opening greetings, or simple greetings between speakers at the beginning of a conversation or discussion are often interrogatives.

English language speakers use many opening greetings, but most are one of two patterns:
1. Greetings that start with **how**
2. Greetings that start with **what**

> Learning to recognize opening greetings and give some of the sample responses below can help make such greetings easier to understand and respond to, even if slightly different patterns or vocabulary are used.

Table 1. Common How Greetings

How are you?	How's everything?	How's life?
How's school?	How's it going?	How are you doing?

How greetings seem to be asking complex questions but are often used in place of a simple *hello*. The person who uses a how greeting generally does not expect a lengthy answer. Similar basic responses can be used for all of them.

It is not accurate to respond to a how greeting with *hello* or *yes*. Use a positive adjective such as *fine*, *good*, *great*, *pretty good*, or *fantastic*. These greetings can be followed by asking a similar question or returning the same question to the asker (e.g., "And you?").

Table 2. Common What Greetings

What's going on?	What's happening?	What's up?
What's new?	What've you been up to?	What'd you do today?

Most responses to **what greetings** consist of one turn or one-and-a-half turns between speakers. Though the listener can add more information, the most common responses are:

> "not too much"
> "nothing"
> "nothing much"

Turn-taking in a conversation often goes back to the respondent: *And you?* or a similar question can be asked in return. Similar to how greetings, these questions are generally recognized as basic greetings.

> It is considered strange to answer "what greetings" too directly or by giving too much personal information.

Rhetorical Questions

A **rhetorical question** is a type of question that does not require an answer.

> Most rhetorical questions are formed in the same manner as other questions, so the listener must use situational clues to recognize the implication or intention of the speaker's question (see Chapters 13 and 14).

One style of rhetorical question that has a different grammatical form is the **un-inverted question**. An un-inverted question is one in which neither the verb nor the *wh*-question word is moved to the head of the sentence. The *wh*-question still appears at the beginning of the sentence if it is used as the determiner of the subject or as a pronoun that is the subject of the sentence.

Un-inverted questions are generally used to express **surprise at new information**. The specific information that the speaker finds surprising is generally marked with a *wh*-question word.

> *Examples of un-inverted questions:*
> You ate **what**?! (the speaker is surprised about what was eaten, not who ate it)
> **Who** ate it?! (the speaker is surprised about who ate it, not what was eaten)
> He looked at **whose** cat?! (the speaker is surprised about the owner of the cat)
> You went to school **how**?! (the speaker is surprised by the method used to get to school)

It is generally not appropriate to actually answer a rhetorical question. If a response *is* given, it is usually a statement of agreement, or a statement made to offer reassurance.

Embedded Questions

In an **embedded question**, the question is placed inside of a statement or another question.

> See Chapter 13 for more information about how embedded questions are used for politeness.

When creating an embedded question, the main question (i.e., the question that the speaker wants answered) must be **un-inverted** because the sentence either becomes a statement, or the grammatical function of asking the question is performed by another part of the sentence.

See the examples and common mistakes below.

> E.g., embedding a question in a statement
> I would like to know <something>+   Where is the bathroom?
> = I would like to know where the bathroom is.
> ~~I would like to know where is the bathroom.~~

> I wonder <something> + Why do you like that?
> = I wonder why you like that.
> ~~I wonder why do you like that.~~

> E.g., embedding a question in another question
> Do you know <something>   + Where is the train station?
> = Do you know where the train station is?
> ~~Do you know where is the train station?~~

> Can you tell me <something>   + Who is the teacher for this class?
> = Can you tell me who the teacher for this class is?
> ~~Can you tell me who is the teacher for this class?~~

When answering an embedded question, be sure to provide the answer that the speaker wants, and not the answer to the grammatical question.

Do you know the answer to the fifth question on the worksheet? → ~~Yes!~~ The answer is 12.

It would be nice if you told me what time it is. → ~~Yes, it would be nice.~~ It's 13:00.

Stating Opinions

Though some questions only require a simple, straight-forward answer (e.g., "What is your student number?"), many questions in academic settings require the speaker to state an opinion based on personal beliefs, understanding, and ideas. In these situations, speakers should begin with a **statement of opinion**, followed by **supporting evidence** and **details**.

There are two types of statement of opinion: **explicit** and **implicit**. Explicit statements of opinion contain personal pronouns, such as *I*, *me*, or *my*, and are more direct. The subject of implicit statements of opinion are not people and are less direct. Tables 3 and 4 show some common phrases used to begin explicit and implicit statements of opinion.

Implicit statements of opinion often use the pronoun *it* or noun phrases like *the evidence*. Implicit statements of opinion distance the speaker from the opinion and create a more neutral stance.

Table 3. Common Phrases for Explicit Statements of Opinion

I think/feel/believe...	In my opinion...	It seems to me that...
I hold the view that...	From my point of view...	In my experience...
As far as I'm concerned...	My impression is that...	The way I see it...

Table 4. Common Phrases for Implicit Statements of Opinion

The evidence suggests that...	It is likely that...	It seems that...
The thing is that...	It makes sense that...	It could be argued that...
It goes without saying...	A case could be made that...	Most people would think...

Statements of opinion can also be strengthened by using adverbs, such as *strongly*, *truly*, and *really*, or weakened by using modal verbs, such as *could*, *may*, or *might*.

> See Chapters 10 and 14 for an explanation of how the strength of adverbs and modal verbs affect the politeness of the statement of opinion.

> *Examples of explicit and implicit statements of opinion:*
> I hold the view that John Jackson will win the next election. (explicit statement)
> I **strongly** hold the view that Jack Johnson will win the next election. (with adverb)
> It seems that John Jackson will win the next election. (implicit statement)
> It seems that John Jackson **might** win the next election. (with modal verb)

When giving your opinion, especially in response to a question, it is not enough to only give a statement of opinion. Instead, evidence and details should be provided to support the opinion or answer to the question. Common types of supporting evidence and details include: reasons, facts and numbers, explanations, and examples.

> The signal words and phrases from Chapter 5, phrases for orally summarizing from Chapter 6, and evidence and clarification vocabulary from Chapter 12 can be used to present evidence and details in a spoken response.

Below are some questions to consider when giving supporting evidence and details for an opinion, and examples of how these questions can help you to think of evidence and details.

Reasons:
→ Why do you think that?
→ Why is that your answer?

(E.g.) I think that school uniforms are bad because they limit freedom.

Explanations:
→ What exactly do you mean by your opinion or response?
→ How does your answer address the question?

(E.g.) When I say that school uniforms limit freedom, I mean that students lose the freedom to choose the clothes that they want to wear.

Facts and Numbers:
→ What background information supports your opinion or answer?

(E.g.) In fact, many schools with school uniform policies do not just limit students' freedom to choose their clothes, but also impose many rules about make-up, hair color, and accessories as well. You ought to know that a survey of students found that 87% of them oppose school uniforms.

Examples:

→ What real-life or imaginary examples show why your opinion is correct?

(E.g.) Take my case. <u>When I was a student, I had to wear a school uniform and it made me feel depressed because I had no choice. Imagine if you had to wear an exact uniform at work regardless of the weather</u>. Wouldn't that make you uncomfortable?

> The more evidence and details that are stated for an opinion, the stronger the argument. For instance, if all of the examples above were used together, it would make a strong argument for being against school uniforms.

Comprehensive Example

 Listen to the audio file on the Pathways Website!

Look at the example of a question and the four responses shown below. Listen to the examples by downloading the audio file from www.pathwaystoacademicenglish.com. Notice that **Answer 4** is the best of the four answers because it provides an appropriate response to the question and provides the most details and evidence for the opinion given.

Question: What do you think is the biggest burden for students when taking online classes?

Answer 1: Yes, I think so.

Answer 2: Yes, it is a burden because it is hard.

Answer 3: The biggest burden is making sure the internet works, because my connection is poor.

Answer 4: It seems that the biggest burden for many students is making sure the internet works. Specifically, though students may have internet at home, those who live in the countryside often don't have fast connections, and those with large families have to share the connection with many others, which slows down their connection. For example, in my house, we have Wi-Fi, but my father and my brother both use it for work, so my connection is often slow when watching videos such as class lectures.

English II-A

Integrated Academic Reading and Writing

Objective 1: Identify the text's organization and logic

9. Connotative and Denotative Meanings
10. Implications and Inferences

Objective 2: Construct an academic paragraph

11. Collocations
12. Paragraph Writing

9. Connotative and Denotative Meanings

Words have two types of meaning: connotative and denotative. The **denotative meaning** is the explicit or direct meaning of a word, sometimes referred to as the "dictionary meaning." On the other hand, the **connotative meaning** of a word is the feeling, implication, or emotion that individuals, cultures, and societies associate with it. Let's look at an example:

> **home** /hoʊm/ *n.*   1. a building where people live.   2. where a person's affections are centered
> **house** /haʊs/ *n.*   1. a building where people live.   2. a household

The words *house* and *home* can both have the denotative meaning of *a place where people live.* *House*, however, only has the meaning of a building or a family, whereas *home* can have connotative meanings of *belonging*, *comfort*, and *safety*.

Understanding both the connotation and denotation of words is important, as it will help students recognize an author's opinion and meaning to accurately identify the argument they are making. Understanding connotations and denotations is also important for understanding inferences and implications (see Chapter 10).

An online or paper dictionary is the best resource for identifying a word's denotative meaning. However, because connotations are often cultural and changeable, one or two sources alone may not provide enough information to determine a word's connotation. As such, you may need to look at several different sources. Four aspects help identify a word's connotative meaning:
1. Degree of meaning
2. Positive or negative association
3. Width of meaning
4. Context

Degree of Meaning

The connotation of a word often expresses the degree of its meaning. For example, the following words all denote the meaning of *bad*. Some are interchangeable in particular phrases, but using a variety of these words can convey varying degrees of dissatisfaction.

lousy / poor	awful / horrible / terrible	atrocious / unacceptable
bad	worse	worst

Language in Action:

Imagine that you hired someone to paint your room, but when you saw the results, you were not satisfied. Below are different ways to describe the poor quality of the painter's work in three different situations.

	Situation	Example Sentence
bad	There's some paint on the floor.	The painter did a **lousy / poor** job.
worse	The painter left dirty rags and paint brushes in your bathroom sink.	What a **horrible / terrible / awful** mess!
worst	You receive a bill for twice as much as you expected.	This service is **atrocious / unacceptable**!

> To identify or guess the connotation of a word, look for multiple examples of words with similar denotative meanings and compare the situations in which they are used.

Table 1 presents words from Table 1 in Chapter 2 that have degree of meaning connotations that are not necessarily obvious from the meaning of the word.

Table 1. List of Synonym Vocabulary with Degree of Meaning Connotations

	Word	Strength and Connotation	Example
1	devote	strong; spend all of one's time, energy or effort	He devoted his life to the study of physics.
2	minimize	strong; to the lowest degree	He minimized his student debt by working three part time jobs.
3	peculiar	strong; very strange	Professor Jones uses a peculiar technique that most people don't ever consider.
4	salvage	strong; after something bad has happened – not before	We thought we had lost all of the data from our experiment, but Professor Smith salvaged it from our broken hard drive.
5	violation	strong	He was arrested for violating ethical guidelines.
6	infraction	weak	He got a fine for a driving infraction.
7	wreak	strong	Free radicals wreak havoc on DNA, causing extensive damage
8	animosity	strong	The professors' rivalry slowly turned into a mutual animosity, and now they won't speak to each other.
9	hurl	strong	The satellite was hurled further into space when it collided with a meteor.

	Word	Strength and Connotation	Example
10	chaotic	strong	Exposing potassium to water causes a chaotic reaction that can destroy laboratory equipment.
11	disorderly	weak	Professor Stevens' room is so disorderly that she has trouble finding her research notes.

Positive or Negative Association

Word choice is an important aspect in both spoken and written language. Some words may have positive or negative associations, while other words may be completely neutral.

Feeling	Example
positive	He is **resolute** in his decision to study biology.
neutral	He is **uncompromising** in his beliefs.
negative	He is **stubborn** about research methods.

In order to determine whether a word has a negative or positive connotation, find several examples of the word used in context and take note of how often it is used in negative and positive situations. If it is used in both, then the connotation is likely neutral. However, if it is primarily used in negative situations, it likely has a negative connotation, and vice versa.

Lost in Translation

When translating between English and Japanese, even if two words have the same denotation, they sometimes have a different connotation. For example, while *urayamashii* and *jealous* have similar denotations, *urayamashii* often has a positive connotation, whereas *jealous* often has a negative connotation. Be careful of English loan words as well, as they often have different connotations in Japanese. For example, although *challenge* is generally used in positive situations in Japanese, it often has a negative connotation in English.

Table 2 presents words from Table 1 in Chapter 2 that have positive or negative connotations that are not necessarily obvious from the meaning of the word.

Table 2. List of Synonym Vocabulary with Positive or Negative Connotation

	Word	Connotation	Example
1	allegedly	negative; implies the alleger might be lying	He allegedly stole his ideas from another researcher.

2	counteract	positive	Iodine can counteract the negative effects of radiation.
3	negate	negative	The mistake in our reporting negated all of our hard work.
4	fad	negative; implies the trend is short lived	I thought his work was good, but it was just a fad.
5	intensify	negative	My headache intensified from the stress of studying.
6	obligation	negative	I want to go home, but I am obligated to help my professor with his research.
7	duty	positive	Teachers have a duty to teach their students.
8	zealot	positive	John is a chemistry zealot.
9	alleviate	positive	The medicine alleviated my headache.

Width of Meaning

Some words can be used in a wide range of situations and therefore have a wide range of meaning. Other words can only be used when certain conditions are met. Therefore, using these words implies that all of the relevant conditions are true. For example, recall that *blurry* and *indistinct* are listed as synonyms in Chapter 2. Though they have the same basic meaning of *not very clear*, *blurry* can only be used when discussing visual stimuli, whereas *indistinct* can be used with any type of stimulus. Therefore, *blurry* is only acceptable in the first example, whereas *indistinct* is acceptable in both.

Example:

We need to conduct the experiment again because the video is too **blurry / indistinct**.

The sound file could not be analyzed because it was too **blurry / indistinct**.

Table 3 presents synonym pairs from Table 1 in Chapter 2 that have different widths of meaning. The word with the wider meaning is given first.

Table 3. List of Synonyms with Width of Meaning Connotation

	Synonym Pair	Difference
1	indistinct / blurry	**blurry** is only used for visual indistinctness (e.g., blurry photos)
2	combination / concoction	**concoction** is usually used for combinations of chemicals or ingredients
3	problem / drawback	**drawback** is only used for negative points of a given topic or subject; **problem** can also refer to a question or inquiry
4	use / employ	**employ** is usually only used for methods, techniques, etc.

	Synonym Pair	Difference
5	search / forage	**forage** is usually used with reference to animals and searching for food, specifically
6	means / medium	**means** can refer to any way of achieving a result (e.g., effort, pen and paper), whereas **medium** is usually only used with a physical means (e.g., pen and paper, copper wires)
7	restart / resume	**resume** implies continuing from the stopping point; **restart** can mean the same *OR* to start again from the beginning
8	proportional / balanced	**proportional** means two things are in the same ratio but not necessarily the same size, while **balanced** implies equal sizes, ratios, or amounts and can be used with many different words
9	void / null	**void** can be used to describe any type of emptiness, but **null** is usually only used in legal or data science contexts
10	freight / cargo	**freight** can refer to shipped goods OR the cost of shipping them; **cargo** is usually only used for goods in large vehicles

Context

As discussed in Chapter 2, the context in which a word is used will determine which of its meanings are relevant. The same is sometimes true for a word's connotation. For example, *white* can have many connotations, including fear, boredom, defeat, and cleanliness.

Connotation	Example
fear	When he heard the wolf howl, his face turned **white** as a sheet.
boredom	Staring at four **white** walls every day drove him crazy.
defeat	The losing army raised a **white** flag and surrendered.
cleanliness	His smile was perfect – with teeth as **white** as snow.

Comprehensive Example

Read the following short passage and answer the questions. Notice how knowledge of the connotative meanings helps you to understand the passage more accurately.

> In order to choose the best synonym for the first question and to better understand the implication of the word *naïve*, identify the connotations of the words the author uses.

Reading Passage

The lost city of Atlantis is a hot topic among some historians. Because the story of Atlantis is so popular with the public, it has attracted the attention of historians, including some who believe that Atlantis actually once existed. As evidence, these researchers often point to texts and maps that suggest where Atlantis might have been located. Nevertheless, other scholars find this group to be rather <u>naïve</u>, because the dated texts and maps they use as evidence have not been corroborated with other properly established documents and maps. Since both groups are unwavering in their respective opinions, it will likely be a long time before this debate is resolved.

1) The word naïve is closest in meaning to:
  (A) kind
  (B) simple
  (C) innocent
  (D) ignorant

2) Which of the following statements can be inferred from the passage?
  (A) Atlantis really existed.
  (B) There is controversy regarding whether or not Atlantis actually existed.
  (C) History is not as serious as other research fields.
  (D) It is clear that Atlantis never existed.

Explanation:
1) Although *naïve* can indeed have meanings such as *kind*, *simple* and *innocent*, in this context, it has a somewhat negative connotation. *Ignorant*, meaning *unknowing* or *ill-informed*, also has a rather negative connotation. Therefore, (D) is the best answer.
2) The author does not offer any evidence as to whether Atlantis existed or not. The passage also does not mention the degree of seriousness regarding this field. The author does, however, state that there is debate over this hot topic. The phrase *hot topic*, in this context, refers to controversy. Therefore, the reader can infer that (B) is the best answer.

See Page 121 for Answers

10. Implications and Inferences

An **implication** is information that a writer or speaker communicates indirectly using connotative word meanings, cultural hints, hedged language, and so on (see Chapters 9 and 13). From a writer's or speaker's **implication,** a listener or reader can make an **inference**. An **inference** is a logical and reasonable conclusion that a reader or listener can reach from the information the writer or speaker has provided, even if that information was not directly stated. For example, if you make dinner for your friends and they say, "...you could be a gourmet cook...," even though they did not say it directly, they are **implying** that the meal you prepared was delicious because they compared you to a gourmet cook. If your friends ask you for second helpings of your dishes, you can **infer** that the meal you prepared was delicious, because if it was not delicious, they probably would not ask for more.

There are three main skills that will help you to make correct inferences:
1. Understanding the writer's or speaker's degree of certainty about a statement
2. Comprehending the logical connections between pieces of information
3. Noticing why the author included certain information

Degree of Certainty

A writer or speaker may use words to express how likely they believe a statement to be true. One way to do this is with adverbs such as *probably, unlikely,* or *possibly* (See Chapter 13). Another way is by using modal verbs. Though modal verbs can be used to convey their standard meanings, they can also be used to imply a writer or speaker's degree of certainty. Below is a list of modal verbs showing both their standard meanings and their implied degree of certainty.

Table 1. Standard Meanings and Implications of Modal Verbs

Modal Verb	Standard Meaning	Implied Degree of Certainty
will	Future tense	100%
would	Imaginary situation / past future tense	about 90%
must	Need	(with evidence) 80%
shall	Suggestion / decision	
should	Better to do	about 70%
may	Permission	about 50%
might		a little less than 50%
can	Ability	(rarely used here)
could	Past ability / imaginary situation	(very low) = 20%

Below is a conversation that shows various degrees of certainty.

> MAN: Will your brother come to the party tonight?
> WOMAN: -He **will** come later. (100% planning on coming)
>
> -He **should** be coming later (he probably will come, but it is not certain)
>
> -He **may** come later (there is about a 50% chance of him coming)
>
> -He **might** come later (the chances that he will not come are slightly higher)
>
> -He **could** come later (there is a very low chance that he will come)

A word's connotation can change a writer's or speaker's implication (see Chapter 9). Recognizing whether a word's connotation is strong or weak, positive or negative, or has changed contextually is an important way to identify a writer's or speaker's implication.

Logical Connection

Understanding the connections between sentences, details, and pieces of information is important to make correct inferences. You can do this by learning the major types of logical connections listed below.

1. chronological (one action happens before/after another)
2. conjunction (both actions happen)
3. disjunction (only one action happens)
4. implication (an action will happen conditionally)
5. cause and effect (one action happens because of another)

Table 2. Words Indicating Logical Connections

Connection	Words	Meaning / Inference
chronological	next, after, later, and then, subsequently, followed by	one thing happens after another (does not indicate cause)
	before, preceded by	one thing happens before another (does not indicate cause)
conjunction	and, and then, moreover, furthermore	both things happen
	but, however, although, even though, despite, in spite of, nevertheless, yet	both things happen, but one is not expected in the circumstances
disjunction	either, or, either but not both, instead, rather, whether	only one of the two things happen (not both, and not neither)
implication	if, then	one thing can only happen if some condition is fulfilled

Connection	Words	Meaning / Inference
implication	no…without	one thing cannot happen unless some condition is not fulfilled
	implies, suggests, points to	one thing *might* mean another thing, but we cannot be 100% sure
cause and effect	because, since, therefore, so, due to, on account of, seeing that, causes, leads to, brings about, yields	one thing happens as a result of the other (the second thing cannot happen without the first thing)
	in order to, so as to, so that, to, for the purpose of	one thing happens for the purpose of causing the second

Below are some examples that exhibit some of the logical connections from Table 2 and their implications.

1. The policy was implemented in several large cities and then <u>subsequently</u> carried out in the countryside as well.

> **Meaning:** The policy was first implemented in urban areas, then later was put into effect in rural areas.
> **Implication:** *It is unknown if the policy being implemented in cities was the cause of it being implemented in the countryside. The implementation in the cities may or may not have influenced its implementation in the countryside.*

2. I was very careful when filling out my application form. <u>Nevertheless,</u> I discovered it had several mistakes after submitting it.

> **Meaning:** I filled out my application form very carefully. The application form had several mistakes.
> **Implication:** *The finding of mistakes was unexpected.*

3. He will <u>either</u> take a physics class <u>or</u> a chemistry class during the first period.

> **Meaning:** He will take a class during the first period. He only has two choices of classes during the first period: physics or chemistry.
> **Implication:** *It is impossible to take both classes during the first period.*

4. <u>No</u> research trips can be taken <u>without</u> the permission of the head professor.

> **Meaning:** Permission from the head professor is required for taking research trips.
> **Implication:** *With the permission of the head professor, it is possible for research trips to be taken, but it is not certain that there will be any research trips.*

5. Changes in policy <u>brought about</u> the tuition increase.

> **Meaning:** The policy changes caused the tuition to increase.
> **Implication:** *If the policy changes did not occur, there would be no increase in tuition.*

Understanding Why Particular Information is Included

Understanding why a writer or speaker has included certain information will help you make inferences about what the main points and supporting details are. As pointed out in Chapters 4 and 5, texts and speeches generally have main ideas. These main ideas are usually found in the first sentences of written paragraphs and are supported by many kinds of details. Some of the common ways to provide details are:

1. illustrating with **examples**
2. **explaining** or describing
3. giving factual **evidence** or reasons
4. contrasting or **refuting** opposing ideas.

> To make correct inferences from a writer's implications, identify the main idea of each paragraph and then connect it to the supporting details in other sentences.

Below is a list of words and phrases that are often used to mark the main types of supporting details.

> **Caution!** Sentences are not always clearly marked with the words in Table 3. Sometimes you will have to rely on your skill of making inferences to determine the relationship between two adjacent sentences.

Table 3. Words that Show How Details are Connected

Examples	Explaining	Evidence	Refuting
illustrates/depicts/ exemplifies…	This means that…	For one…	…misses/ takes for granted/ misinterprets…
For example, … / such as…	In other words…	…provides/gives support for…	…doesn't take <something> into account
…including X, Y, Z.	because/so/therefore/ …	…shows that…	However/but/though/while /contrary to
…from X to Z	specifically/i.e.	…is clear from the fact that…	Conversely/in contrast

Comprehensive Example

Read the following short passage and answer the questions. Notice that recognizing the degree of certainty, identifying logical connections, and understanding why particular information is included helps you to understand the passage more accurately.

In order to understand the inference in the passage, find the logical connections between the information. In order to understand why the author included certain information, check Table 3 for words that show how details are connected.

Reading Passage

Compounds are substances that are composed of two or more chemically bound elements. There are several types of chemical compounds, but scientists generally classify all compounds as being either organic or inorganic. A compound is considered organic if it contains a carbon atom that is bound to hydrogen. For example, sucrose, a type of sugar, contains a carbon atom that is bound to both hydrogen and oxygen, and is therefore classified as organic. Conversely, elements that do not have a carbon atom, or contain carbon atoms that are not bound to hydrogen, are considered inorganic. For example, carbon dioxide contains a carbon atom, but its atom is only bound to oxygen. Organic compounds are usually associated with biochemistry because all known life is built upon the carbon-hydrogen (C-H) bond structure. On the other hand, inorganic compounds are generally associated with non-living materials. However, inorganic compounds can be present in organic material – sometimes in abundance – and can be necessary for life despite their chemical structure lacking C-H bonds.

1) What can be inferred from the passage?

(A) Compounds require at least two elements to be considered organic.

(B) Oxygen is required for living organisms.

(C) Carbon dioxide is not an organic compound.

(D) Some organic compounds lack carbon atoms.

2) Why did the author include the last sentence?

(A) To give examples of the types of living organisms.

(B) To explain why C-H bonds are so necessary in organic chemistry.

(C) To provide evidence that inorganic compounds exist in organic material.

(D) To refute the idea that inorganic compounds are only associated with non-living material.

Explanation:

1) The author does not directly state that carbon dioxide is inorganic. However, the author does say that compounds can only be classified as organic if they contain a carbon atom bound to hydrogen. The passage then states that carbon dioxide lacks a C-H bond. Furthermore, the author uses carbon dioxide as a contrasting example to the organic compound, sucrose. Therefore, (C) is the best answer.

2) The author explains that organic compounds are generally associated with living things whereas inorganic compounds are generally associated with non-living things. However, the author then uses the word *however*, and states that inorganic compounds can be present in organic material and necessary for life, which seems contrary to the idea that inorganic compounds are generally associated with non-living things. Therefore, (D) is the best answer.

See Page 121 for Answers

11. Collocations

Collocations are simply "words that go together." Native speakers of English use and expect these pairings, and inappropriate pairings may sound unnatural or be grammatically incorrect.

For example, the verb *to commit* can have the same meaning as *to do*, but it usually goes with words that have negative connotations, such as *crime*. Therefore, *commit* (not *do*) would be used in sentences **A** and **B**, and *do* (not *commit*) would be used in sentences **C** and **D**.

(A) The terrorists will **commit** acts of violence unless they are stopped.

(B) The crime was **committed** by a cunning thief.

(C) Our community **does** neighborhood clean-up once a month.

(D) I'll be busy all day **doing** tasks to get ready for the conference.

Remembering collocations will help you to write paragraphs with fewer errors, and process English more quickly when reading academic texts or listening to lectures.

Common Collocations

There are four frequently-used verbs that combine with nouns or noun phrases to create collocations: **do**, **have**, **make**, and **take**.

Table 1. Verbs Commonly Used in Collocations

Verb	Meaning Sense	Noun Phrase		
		+indefinite article	+definite article	no article
do	perform a task	a chore	the job	homework
have	host or possess	a meeting	the chance	trouble
make	create, devise, be accepted	a judgment	the team	arrangements
take	engage in, accept, support	a position	the time	responsibility

Other collocations use other verbs, or are combinations of verbs and particles such as *to* and *as*. Study the list of common collocations used in academic English in Table 2. The words in (parentheses) are generally needed but not required in all circumstances.

Table 2. Common Collocations in Academic English

	Headword	Common Collocations
1	achieve	achieve a goal, achieve an objective, achieve an outcome
2	address	address an issue
3	adopt	adopt (an) approach, adopt (a) procedure, be widely adopted
4	arrangement	make arrangements
5	attempt	make an attempt
6	authority	exercise authority (over <someone>)
7	clue	give a clue, provide a clue (about <something>)
8	collect	collect data, collect information
9	comment	make a comment (about <something>)
10	commit	commit an offense, commit a crime, commit to <doing something>
11	conduct	conduct research, conduct an experiment, conduct a survey
12	conference	attend a conference, hold a conference
13	convey	convey a message, convey information, convey (a) meaning
14	correct	correct an error, correct a mistake
15	deal	deal with (an issue/problem/etc.)
16	deem	deem <something> (in)appropriate, deem <something> necessary
17	demonstrate	demonstrate competence, be (clearly) demonstrated
18	doubt	cast doubt on <something>
19	engage	engage in (an activity)
20	enhance	(greatly) enhance performance
21	face	face a challenge, face a dilemma, face a problem, face difficulty, face discrimination
22	fall into	fall into the category (of), fall into a number of categories
23	follow	follow instructions, follow the law, follow the rules
24	format	follow a format, use a format, standard format
25	gain	gain access (to), gain information, gain insight (into)
26	impression	create an impression, make an impression, give <someone> an impression
27	initial	initial period, initial phase, initial stage
28	insight	gain insight, give insight, offer insight, provide insight (into)
29	interview	conduct an interview
30	judgment	make a judgment
31	message	convey a message, deliver a message
32	obligation	have an obligation, fulfill an obligation
33	observation	make a/an (direct) observation
34	obtain	obtain a result, obtain data, obtain information

	Headword	Common Collocations
35	opportunity	create an opportunity, offer an opportunity, provide an opportunity
36	overview	provide an overview, give an overview
37	parameter	set (the) parameters
38	perform	perform a function, perform an operation, perform a task
39	pose	pose a challenge, pose a problem, pose a question, pose a threat (to)
40	precede	take precedence (over), preceding chapter, preceding section
41	present	present an argument, present a challenge, present a summary, present data, present evidence
42	presentation	give a presentation
43	priority	give priority (to)
44	procedure	adopt a procedure, follow a procedure, use a procedure
45	raise	raise an issue, raise a question, raise awareness
46	range	cover a range (of), the entire range (of), the full range (of)
47	reach	reach an agreement, reach consensus, reach a peak
48	recommend	make a recommendation
49	refer	be (commonly) referred to (as)
50	regard	be (widely) regarded (as)
51	rely	rely on
52	require	meet a (minimum) requirement
53	research	conduct research (on), carry out research (on)
54	resemblance	bear a resemblance (to), bear no resemblance (to)
55	resolve	resolve (a) conflict, resolve a dispute
56	responsible	accept responsibility (for), assume responsibility (for), take responsibility (for), be (directly /partly/primarily) responsible (for)
57	result	obtain a result, result in
58	role	play a role, take on a role, assume the role (of), take the role (of)
59	seek	seek help, seek information
60	seem	seem (in)appropriate, seem obvious, seem plausible
61	sense	in a (literal/figurative) sense
62	serve	serve a function
63	set	set a goal, set an objective, set the agenda, set (the) parameters
64	strategy	develop a strategy, have a strategy
65	suit	be suited to, be suited for
66	support	support an argument
67	task	carry out a task, complete a task, perform a task
68	technique	develop a technique, employ a technique, use a technique
69	tendency	exhibit a tendency, have a tendency, show a (strong) tendency (to)

	Headword	Common Collocations
70	theory	develop a theory, test a theory
71	topic	cover a topic, discuss a topic, related topic, research topic
72	treatment	give <someone> (preferential/special) treatment, receive treatment
73	vested	(have a) vested interest in <something>

When studying collocations, look at several examples of each collocation being used in a sentence and learn both the denotative meaning and the connotative meaning (see Chapter 9).

Commonly Misused Collocates

Below is a list of words that are often used incorrectly by Japanese learners of English. Be careful not to make these mistakes when writing.

Table 3. Commonly Misused Collocates

Headword	Incorrect Collocation and Explanation
by	cut ~~by~~ scissors (*With* should be used for tools or instruments.)
challenge	~~challenge~~ a solution to the problem (*Challenge* cannot be used for attempts. Use *try* instead.)
grow	My parents ~~grew me up~~. (*Grow* is transitive and not used for humans. Use *raise* instead.) (*Grow up* can be used for humans, but is intransitive.)
how	~~How~~ do you think? (This is the incorrect question word. Use *what* instead.)
meet	~~meet an accident~~ (Accidents cannot be met. Use *get into an accident* or *have an accident* instead.)
narrow	His apartment is too ~~narrow~~. (*Narrow* can be used for corridors, hallways and other paths, but generally note for rooms or whole buildings. Use *small* instead.)
open	~~open a meeting~~ (*Open a meeting* means to start a meeting. Use *have* or *hold a meeting* to mean that the meeting is taking place.)
play	~~play running/skiing/etc.~~ (*Play* is usually only used for sports or games that have scored points. For races and judged competitions, use *do*, or use the name of the sport itself if it is recognized as a verb.)

Headword	Incorrect Collocation and Explanation
to	attend ~~to~~ class, turn ~~to~~ cold, go ~~to~~ back home, walk ~~to~~ up the stairs (*to* is unnecessary with *attend*, *turn*, and *home*; it is also unnecessary in most phrasal verbs of motion)
wish	I ~~wish~~ he will win. (*wish* is generally used for desires that are impossible or unlikely to happen; use *hope* for desires that are possible or likely to happen)
with	marry ~~with~~ <someone>, date ~~with~~ <someone> (*with* is not required with these verbs)

Comprehensive Example

Read the passage below that contains several of the common collocations that were introduced in this chapter. Choose the word that best fills in each blank.

> In order to find the answers to the questions, check the common collocations listed in Table 2.

Reading Passage

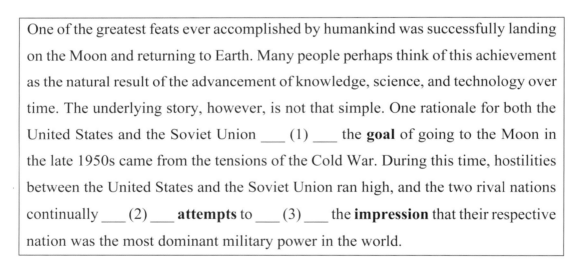

One of the greatest feats ever accomplished by humankind was successfully landing on the Moon and returning to Earth. Many people perhaps think of this achievement as the natural result of the advancement of knowledge, science, and technology over time. The underlying story, however, is not that simple. One rationale for both the United States and the Soviet Union ____ (1) ____ the **goal** of going to the Moon in the late 1950s came from the tensions of the Cold War. During this time, hostilities between the United States and the Soviet Union ran high, and the two rival nations continually ____ (2) ____ **attempts** to ____ (3) ____ the **impression** that their respective nation was the most dominant military power in the world.

1) (A) looking (B) setting (C) aiming (D) targeting
2) (A) had   (B) made   (C) tried   (D) aimed
3) (A) create   (B) have   (C) present (D) show

See Page 121 for Answers

12. Paragraph Writing

A paragraph contains a series of related sentences that deal with a single topic. Longer texts contain a series of related paragraphs that develop each single topic into one coherent theme. Therefore, the ability to write a good paragraph must be mastered in order to effectively write longer papers such as essays, theses, and research reports.

> Recognizing a paragraph's structure can also give clues about where keywords, topic sentences, and supporting information are located, which helps with skimming and scanning (see Chapter 3).

There are four main things to keep in mind when writing a paragraph:
1. **structure**
2. adequate **evidence**
3. proper **connection** of ideas
4. **variation**

Paragraph Structure

All good English paragraphs share a similar structure. They begin with an introductory sentence called a topic sentence, which describes the main idea of the paragraph. The topic sentence is followed by several supporting sentences, which further develop the idea. The paragraph ends with either a concluding or a transition sentence. A paragraph should be unified, meaning that all of the sentences should support the main idea as presented in the topic sentence. A paragraph is considered coherent if each sentence flows smoothly into the next without shifting to irrelevant or unrelated information. A good paragraph also clearly connects previous information with new information. The basic structure of a paragraph is shown here:

1. Topic Sentence

2. Supporting Sentence 1
Supporting Sentence 2
…etc.

3. Transition or Concluding
Sentence

The **topic sentence** clearly states the topic, purpose, or main idea of the paragraph. When writing a topic sentence, the idea should not be too general because if it is, the topic may not be able to be discussed in a single paragraph. It is equally important that the idea is not too specific because if it is, supporting information to further develop the topic may be unnecessary.

Compare the following topic sentence examples:

(A) My Japanese school uniform is very stylish. **(only personal opinion)**
(B) Japanese school uniforms reflect various aspects of Japanese culture. **(too general)**
(C) Fairness is one of the benefits associated with Japanese school uniforms. **(good)**
(D) Japanese school uniforms, adopted in the Meiji era, violate the human right of self-expression. **(has too many main ideas)**

Sentence **A** expresses a personal opinion rather than an idea that could be expanded upon, so it is not a good example of a topic sentence. Sentence **B** is too general to be a topic sentence because it does not mention any aspects of Japanese culture around which the paragraph can be built. This means that multiple paragraphs will be needed to develop the topic. Sentence **C** is a good topic sentence because it is neither too general nor too specific. It clearly expresses the idea that fairness is a benefit of school uniforms. It invites supporting information by indicating that there are other benefits of school uniforms. Sentence **D** is a poor topic sentence because it includes two main ideas, which need to be separated into at least two paragraphs.

Supporting Sentences and Evidence

Supporting sentences further develop the idea captured in a topic sentence. Supporting sentences can provide *evidence* for the main idea or *clarification* of the main idea. Evidence includes reasons, examples, statistics, and other factual data that support the idea. Clarifications include explanations, definitions of important terms, and classifications.

Table 1. Evidence and Clarification Vocabulary

Introducing Reasons	it should be noted that… …due to (the fact that) … …is based on… it follows that…	factors of this… consequently… the reason for/why… for one…
Introducing Examples	for instance for example to illustrate as can be seen by	including… such as… in the case that… … (e.g., A, B, C, and D)

Introducing Numbers	a wide range of there are a number of as a matter of fact	the results/chart/ study show(s) that...
Introducing Counter-arguments	while/though... on the other hand...	...does not take into account... ...but at the same time
Providing Explanation	specifically in other words... with respect to... as explained by...	... (i.e., ...) this means that... ...(be) considered as...
Providing Definitions	...(be) regarded as... ...means / ..., meaning ..., also known as...	what is called... refers to...
Providing Classification	to distinguish between A and B... the difference between A and B... A and B fall into...	A and B are divided into... A and B can be categorized...

> If a paragraph's supporting sentences are irrelevant or only weakly connected to the topic sentence, the paragraph will be unclear. When writing a paragraph, ensure that all sentences relate clearly to the topic sentence. If they do not, then create a new paragraph for those sentences.

Be sure to avoid **fallacies** in supporting sentences. A fallacy is a mistake in reasoning or thinking that leads to inappropriate evidence. Note that just because something is a fallacy does not necessarily mean that it is untrue. Below are some fallacies to avoid:

1. Claiming that there are only two options when in fact there are many.
   Example: "If you don't support the prime minister's policies, you hate him."
   Explanation: It is possible to support only some of the prime minister's policies and still like him. Similarly, it is possible to support some of his policies and hate him.

2. <u>Claiming that one thing will cause other things to happen without sufficient evidence.</u>

Example: "If you let one student drink cola in class, soon every student will be doing it."

Explanation: This outcome is indeterminable from this statement alone. Maybe some other students will drink cola in class, but it is also possible that other students have no interest in drinking cola in class.

3. <u>Defending a claim by repeating it.</u>

Example: "Plants need water to live because without water they can't live."

Explanation: It is true that plants need water to live, but this sentence just repeats the fact twice. This statement provides no evidence of what water does to keep plants alive.

4. <u>Claiming that something is correct because everyone says so or is doing it.</u>

Example: "This new diet is probably effective because many people are trying it."

Explanation: People often do popular things. The fact that many people are trying the diet is not proof of its effectiveness.

5. <u>Changing another person's claim so that it is easy to make a counter-argument.</u>

Example: "John says that he doesn't want to study physics, but I think he is wrong to hate science."

Explanation: John does not say that he hates science. He says he does not want to study physics, not all science. Furthermore, this statement does not even necessarily mean that John dislikes physics.

Connecting Ideas

In academic writing, it is important to connect sentences and paragraphs properly. Having too many short sentences without logical connection vocabulary will confuse the reader. Be sure to use vocabulary that connects sentences appropriately and clearly shows the logical connections between ideas (see Chapter 10). This way it is clear how evidence is connected to other evidence or to the main idea of the paragraph.

Unclear connection between ideas and sentences:

I think that courage is important in life. I was afraid to study abroad. I decided to study abroad.

Clear connection between ideas and sentences:

I think that courage is important in life, which <u>led me to</u> study abroad <u>even though</u> I was afraid to.

Paragraphs should end with either a transition sentence or a concluding sentence. **Transition sentences** lead the reader to the next paragraph by connecting the main idea presented in one paragraph to a new main idea presented in the next paragraph. In contrast, **concluding sentences** are used at the end of a section of text to summarize the important points in the paragraph.

Variation

In English writing, it is important not to overuse the same words or phrases in a single paragraph or sentence. Good writers make use of a variety of words and phrases to better illustrate their ideas. Using synonyms (see Chapter 2) and paraphrases (see Chapter 4) instead of repeating words and phrases used earlier in the paragraph can help improve variation and increase clarity. Furthermore, when providing evidence and making logical connections, be sure to use a variety of vocabulary from the tables in this chapter and those from Chapter 10.

Comprehensive Example

Read the paragraph below. Notice how it follows the general paragraph structure outlined above, presents a good amount of evidence and clarification vocabulary (in **bold**), and employs synonyms for variation.

Example Paragraph

Hydraulic fracturing, **also known as** *fracking*, can **bring about** great economic benefits to local communities, but its environmental and health costs outweigh them. Hydraulic fracturing **refers to** an oil and gas extraction process by which highly pressurized water, sand, ceramic beads, and chemicals are injected deep into the earth, causing subterranean rock formations to crack and **subsequently** release the gas and oil deposits they contain. **It should be noted that** fracking, **with respect to** traditional extraction techniques, is highly effective. Without fracking, otherwise out-of-reach oil and gas would remain trapped underground. **Consequently,** the technique effectively increases the supply of much-needed fossil fuels. **In addition**, fracking is labor-intensive and therefore its drilling operations provide hundreds of jobs to the local communities near fracking sites. **However,** these advantages **do not take into account** the environmental hazards posed by this extracting method. **For one**, there has been the highly publicized issue of earthquakes being caused by the insertion of wastewater back into the ground. These man-made seismic events have been recorded at virtually all locations where hydraulic fracturing has taken place. **Furthermore**, once a fracking well has run dry, the chemical-laden fluids remain behind, contaminating the surrounding soil which can

bring about serious health risks. **Specifically**, more than two dozen chemicals, including toluene, ethylbenzene, and xylene, which are proven carcinogens, are used in the fracking process. **Moreover**, fracking causes airborne pollutants to be released into the atmosphere, which compromises the regional air quality. **For instance**, dangerous amounts of methane, sulfur oxide, and benzene have been recorded at fracking locations. **Therefore**, strict rules, regulations, and safeguards need to be instituted before hydraulic fracturing can be considered as a viable option for unearthing petroleum products.

Explanation:

In this example, the topic sentence clearly outlines the idea that the disadvantages of fracking outweigh any advantages it has. The supporting sentences plainly define the topic and give examples that support the idea. The paragraph uses many pieces of evidence and utilizes a wide variety of evidence and clarification vocabulary from this chapter and words from Tables 2 and 3 of Chapter 10. In addition, there is variation in the paragraph's vocabulary and style. For example, though there are few synonyms for *fracking*, the paragraph uses several variations to describe the water used in fracking, such as *fluid*, *wastewater*, and *hydraulic*. Similarly, the paragraph uses *fossil fuels* and *petroleum products* as synonyms for *oil and natural gas*. Finally, the paragraph concludes with a transition sentence that allows the next paragraph to introduce a new main idea specifically about rules and regulations related to fracking

English II-B

Integrated Academic Speaking and Listening

Objective 1: Understand a speaker's intent

13. Indirect Language
14. Tone of Voice

Objective 2: Discuss academic topics

15. Fluency and Pronunciation
16. Discussion Strategies

13. Indirect Language

Speakers use **indirect language** for politeness or to show uncertainty, often to accomplish a specific goal (e.g., **suggesting**, **requesting**, **refusing**, and **apologizing**). While direct language usually has a clear purpose, indirect language is typically less clear. Consider the two examples below.

> **Direct:** I won't join you today.
> **Indirect:** I'm afraid that it would be difficult for me to join you today.

In the direct sentence, it is obvious that the purpose of the statement is refusal. It indicates that the speaker will not accompany the listener. In contrast, the intention of the indirect sentence is less clear, but it is more polite.

This chapter explains how to use **context clues**, and knowledge of **hedging** and **common indirect phrases** to understand the goal of a speaker using indirect language.

Politeness

English speakers often use **indirect language** for the sake of **politeness**. In general, the more indirect an expression is, the more polite it is considered to be. However, English does not have specific verb forms that indicate politeness, like *sonkeigo*, *kenjougo*, and *teineigo* in Japanese. Instead, a variety of indirect expressions can be used to mark politeness in English. It is helpful to understand the situations in which English speakers are likely to use indirect language for the sake of politeness.

In most English-speaking countries, people tend to use polite language with a person who is in a position of authority. Therefore, you are likely to hear indirect language in conversations where one person is in a position of authority over the other. Examples include conversations between a student and a university professor, an employee and their boss, or a student and a member of university staff.

> Listen for one speaker using a title before someone's surname (e.g., **Mr.** Stevens, **Ms.** Smith, **Dr.** Johnson, and **Professor** Brown) or an honorific (e.g., *sir* or *ma'am*). The use of titles or honorifics is a clue that one person is recognizing the other's social status or position of authority and is therefore likely to use indirect language in order to be polite.

Across the globe, most English speakers tend to be polite when speaking with strangers. Certain verbal clues indicate when two people do not know each other. Expressions such as ***excuse me*** or ***pardon me*** are often used to start a conversation with a stranger or get a stranger's attention. When these expressions are used, the speakers are likely to use indirect language with each other.

Culturally, most English speakers tend not to use polite language with classmates or colleagues, regardless of their age (i.e., in these cultures, there is no concept of *senpai* and *kohai*). Therefore, two friends would likely not use titles or surnames when addressing each other. However, English speakers do use indirect language even with people who are close to them if they must make a difficult request or communicate bad news.

Interpreting Indirect Language: Taking Clues from Context

When interpreting indirect language, it is important to consider the context – the connection between what is said and the content of the other parts of the conversation. If the meaning of a phrase is not clear from its literal interpretation, consider the following questions:

What is the relationship between the speakers?
What does the speaker want the listener to do?
What information do the speaker and the listener(s) share?
What is the speaker's attitude towards the listener or situation?

Language in Action:
Imagine that someone says "Let's not talk about what happened last week." This could mean several things depending on what the speaker did last week or what they know about what happened. Because the speaker does not want to talk about it, we can probably assume that *what happened last week* was something negative or possibly embarrassing. Here are other assumptions we can make depending on the context:

- Unless the conversation continues or the listener has additional information about the incident, it is not clear why the participants should not talk about what happened.
- Without additional knowledge, you might be able to infer certain points by paying attention to the speaker's tone of voice, facial expressions, and clues from the environment.
- If the speaker seems embarrassed, ashamed, secretive, or angry, you can infer that the incident was something negative.
- If the speaker seems light-hearted or simply shy, we can guess that the incident may not have been so serious.

Interpreting Indirect Language: Hedging

Hedging is a technique often used to make language more indirect and therefore more polite. A variety of words can be used for hedging. When hedging words are paired with indirect expressions in spoken English, they soften a statement and make it more polite. Alternatively, hedging words can be used to reduce the strength or certainty with which an idea is proposed in either spoken or written language. Four types of words or phrases used for hedging are:

1. Modal verbs
2. Weak verbs
3. Words and phrases that show uncertainty
4. Dummy subjects

Modal verbs are often used in hedging. In the examples below, notice that adding a modal verb weakens the statement, and using weaker modal verbs makes the statement more polite.

> I **want** your help tomorrow. (certain)
>
> I **may want** your help tomorrow. (less certain; your help might not be needed)
>
> You **should** study harder for tomorrow's test. (high certainty modal verb, not as polite)
>
> You **may want to** study harder for tomorrow's test. (low certainty modal verb, more polite)

> Refer to Table 1 (Standard Meanings and Implications of Modal Verbs) in Chapter 10. Use of modal verbs that express less certainty make an expression more polite.

Weak verbs imply less certainty or have a weaker connotation than strong verbs. For example, the verbs in Table 1 are often used in hedging because of their weak connotations. These verbs are typically followed by *that*.

Table 1. Verbs Commonly Used in Hedges

Verb	Example
appear	It **appears** that more studying time is correlated with higher grades.
assume	I **assume** that he has done enough background research.
believe	It is **believed** to be a valid way of reducing flooding in the area.
doubt	I **doubt** that there is enough evidence to say that for sure.
indicate	Previous studies **indicate** that drinking water reduces the chance of getting headaches.
mention	I **mentioned** that he wanted to participate last week.
seem	It **seems** that ultraviolet radiation can kill most bacteria.
suggest	The data **suggests** that high cholesterol increases the risk of a heart attack.

> Refer to Chapter 9 for an explanation of connotation. Words with weaker connotations are usually used in more polite expressions.

Another common type of hedging involves the use of **words that show uncertainty**. Below is a table of words that show uncertainty and examples of these words in use.

Table 2. Common Words Used to Show Uncertainty

Word (family)	Example
conceivable, conceivably	**Conceivably**, the results of this study can advance our understanding of physics.
hope, hopeful, hopefully	It is **hoped** that this discovery will benefit society.
kind of	I **kind of** want to join your study session.
likelihood, (un)likely	The **likelihood** of his theory being true is low.
possible, possibly, possibility	There is a **possibility** that I will join you.
probable, probably, probability	It is **probable** that global warming affects our lives now.
to some degree / extent, somewhat	I think it is an important work, **to some extent**.

> Many of the words in Table 2 can appear in hedges as various parts of speech, so it is best to remember them as word families (see Chapter 2).

Finally, the use of a **dummy subject** (*it* or *there* when not connected to a particular entity, e.g., *it is raining*) neutralizes the sentence, making the statement less direct and often more polite.

> More than one hedge can be used in a single expression. The more indirectness and hedging a sentence includes, the more polite or less certain it seems.

Language in Action:

Imagine that you want to ask to join a professor's laboratory. All of the expressions below have the same basic meaning, but varying amounts of hedging and thus different levels of politeness.

Please let me join your laboratory. (direct request, not rude, but not very polite)
I **was hoping you would** let me join your laboratory. (+ indirectness)
I was hoping you **might** let me join your laboratory. (+ weaker modal verb)
I was hoping that you might **possibly** let me join your laboratory. (+ uncertainty)

The final sentence is very polite because it employs two **words that show uncertainty** (*hope* and *possibly*) and uses a **weak modal verb** (*might* instead of *would*). The first sentence is not rude, but it does not use any indirectness or hedging, so it is not very polite, either.

Language in Action:

Imagine that you are reading the results of a research paper about acupuncture. All of the sentences below have a similar meaning but show varying amounts of hedging and thus different levels of uncertainty.

> Acupuncture **is** an effective method of treating chronic pain.
> (very confident)
> Acupuncture **could be** an effective method of treating chronic pain.
> (+ modal verb)
> Acupuncture could **possibly** be an effective method of treating chronic pain.
> (+ uncertainty)
> **It seems that** acupuncture could possibly be an effective method of treating chronic pain.
> (+ dummy subject, + weak verb)

The final sentence shows the least amount of certainty because it employs four types of hedging: a **weak verb** (*seem*), a **dummy subject** (*it*), a weak **modal verb** (*could*), and a **word that shows uncertainty** (*possibly*). Conversely, the first sentence contains no hedging and therefore makes a strong claim about the effectiveness of acupuncture.

Research reports tend to use hedging, especially in their concluding sections, because it is always possible that a study is flawed. Therefore, scientific papers use hedging to varying degrees, depending on how convincing the data is, whether or not it matches the data of other studies, and how well it supports the paper's conclusion.

Interpreting Indirect Language: Common Indirect Phrases

The following four types of speech usually contain indirect phrases because they either have the potential to irritate or offend the listener, or are used when the listener is already offended:

1. Indirect suggestions
2. Indirect requests
3. Indirect refusals
4. Apologies and non-apologies

1. Indirect Suggestions

Suggestions include giving advice, issuing invitations, and making statements of disapproval or criticism. Note that advice and recommendations are usually **positive**, whereas disapproval and criticism are often **negative**. Indirect suggestions can be categorized into three basic types:

- Rhetorical questions
- Advice directed at others
- Subjunctive suggestions

Rhetorical questions can be used to make suggestions. In this case, the speaker expects the listener to follow the advice rather than answer the question.

> Rhetorical questions are interrogatives to which the speaker does not expect an answer. They can also be used to express surprise or disappointment. (See Chapter 8)

Advice directed at others involves the speaker making a general suggestion or directing their suggestion to a large group or category to which the listener belongs. Though the speaker does not name the listener, in particular, they usually expect the listener to realize that they belong to the group or category being addressed and thus that they should follow the advice.

Subjunctive suggestions involve using conditional language (e.g., *if* and *when*) or the subjunctive mood (e.g., *would* and *could*) to talk about a hypothetical situation or counterfactual. Table 3 shows the most common phrases for making indirect suggestions and examples.

Table 3. Common Phrases Used in Indirect Suggestions

Type	Expression	Example
rhetorical questions	Why not… / Why don't you...?	**Why not** use the lab manual?
	Have you / Did you…?	**Have you** tried visiting the student learning center?
advice directed at others	should / had better	Students **shouldn't** cheat on their tests.
	the best way to…	**The best way to** study for the test is to work through the practice test.
	It could / might be…	**It might be** a good idea to study harder.
subjunctive suggestions	If I were you	I wouldn't do that **if I were you**.
	You might want to…	**You might want to** close the door after you leave.
	If you think about it…	**If you think about it**, there is only one thing you can do.

2. Indirect Requests

Requests include asking for favors, giving orders, and issuing warnings. The social status of a speaker determines whether they can issue orders and give warnings. Usually, only speakers in a position of authority can do so. Indirect requests can be categorized into four basic types:

- Embedded questions
- Acknowledging the listener's trouble
- Emphasizing the speaker's feelings
- Subjunctive requests

An **embedded question** is a polite request in which the speaker hides the real request by placing it inside of another question or statement. Embedded questions allow the listener to refuse the request with a short reply, explanation, or apology. For example:

> **Embedded Question:** Do you know what time it is?
> →*No, sorry, I don't have a watch.*
> →*Sorry, I don't know the time.*

See Chapter 8 for more information about how to create and respond to embedded questions.

Acknowledging the listener's trouble involves the speaker using an expression that demonstrates recognition that their request might burden or impose on the listener in some way.

Emphasizing the speaker's feelings is a way of encouraging the listener to act by asking them to consider how the speaker will feel if they accept the request (i.e., positive) or decline it (i.e., negative).

Subjunctive requests are like subjunctive suggestions in that they involve using conditional language (e.g., *if* and *when*) or the subjunctive mood (e.g., *would* and *could*) to talk about a hypothetical situation.

Table 4 shows the most common phrases for making indirect requests and examples.

Table 4. Common Phrases Used in Indirect Requests

Type	Expression	Example
embedded questions	Do you think / know…	**Do you think** you could help me?
	I wonder (if)	**I wonder** if you could help me.
acknowledging the listener's trouble	…too much trouble…	If it's not **too much trouble**, please help me with my homework.

Type	Expression	Example
	I hate to ask, but…	**I hate to ask, but** will you lend me your textbook until next week?
	Can / could…	**Can** you come by later, or are you busy?
emphasizing the speaker's feelings	It would be nice…	**It would be nice** if you turned your homework in on time.
	I was hoping…	**I was hoping** you would help me.
subjunctive requests	Would you like to…	**Would you like to** help me later?
	Would you mind…	**Would you mind** turning in your report early?

3. Indirect Refusals

Refusals include declining various types of **suggestions** and **requests**. Refusals involve rejecting the listener in some way, and thus speakers often use indirectness when making a refusal to prevent offending the listener. Indirect refusals can be categorized into three basic types:

- Expressing regret
- Giving excuses or reasons
- Pointing to uncertainty or discomfort

When **expressing regret**, the speaker indicates that they are sorry to refuse or that they wish they did not have to.

Giving excuses or reasons so that the listener will not blame the speaker or be angry with them is common when refusing. In indirect refusals, specific words of refusal (e.g., *no, I will not*) are often omitted and the excuse alone is understood to be a refusal.

When **pointing to uncertainty or discomfort**, the speaker expects the listener to infer that they are refusing, without actually using specific words of refusal. Speakers can accomplish this by claiming to be unsure or mentioning the burden that complying with the request would place on them.

> Tone of voice helps to signal that uncertain words or phrases, such as *could* or *I don't know*, should be understood to be refusals (see Chapter 13).

Table 5 shows the most common phrases for making indirect refusals and examples.

Table 5. Common Phrases Used in Indirect Refusals

Type	Expression	Example
expressing regret	If only…	**If only** I didn't have class at that time.
	I wish…	**I wish** I could go, but I have other plans.
giving excuses or reasons	I already…	**I already** promised my mother I would help her.
	The thing is…	**The thing is**, I've already made other plans.
	Don't worry about it (reason)	**Don't worry about it**, I have enough people to help me.
pointing to uncertainty or discomfort	I'm not sure… / I don't know (if)…	**I'm not sure if** that's a good idea.

4. Apologies and Non-Apologies

Speakers make **apologies** when they have done something that they fear might upset the listener or when they have already offended the listener. Apologies often include an indirect expression to increase politeness. Furthermore, they often, but do not always include a word that shows remorse, such as *sorry*. Apologies can be categorized into four basic types:

- Acknowledging responsibility
- Explaining
- Expressing concern for the listener
- Making offers or promises

Acknowledging responsibility means that the speaker is accepting that they did something wrong.

Explaining is a way for the speaker to reduce the listener's anger by showing that they did their best in the situation and do not wish to offend the listener.

Expressing concern for the listener means that the speaker sympathizes with the listener and expresses remorse regarding the situation.

Making offers or promises is an attempt by the speaker to remedy the situation by doing or promising to do something to help the listener or ensure that the mistake will not happen again.

Table 6 shows the most common indirect phrases for making apologies and examples.

Table 6. Common Indirect Phrases Used in Apologies

Type	Expression	Example
acknowledging responsibility	I'll admit... (should have)	**I'll admit** that I should have checked the logbook before consulting you.
	(self-insult)	I can't believe **I was so inconsiderate**!
	I apologize / my mistake	**I apologize.** That was **my mistake**.
explaining	you (can) see...	I tried to help, but **you can see** I don't have much free time.
	...didn't realize...	Oh, I **didn't realize** you were busy.
	didn't mean to	Sorry, I **didn't mean to**! (it was an accident)
expressing concern for the listener	I know (that) ...	**I know that** you must be angry with me.
making offers or promises	...won't happen again	Don't worry, it **won't happen again**.
	do you want me (to) ...	**Do you want me** to talk to the professor for you?
	...if you want...	Oops! I can fix it **if you want**.
	...but I can / will...	I'm so sorry I broke it, **but I can** get you a new one.
	I'll tell you what... (offer)	**I'll tell you what**, I will pay for the second half.

Be aware that even if an expression includes the word *sorry*, it may simply be expressing **sympathy** and is therefore not necessarily an apology. There are three basic strategies for making such non-apologies:

- Non-acceptance
- Justification
- Shifting blame

Non-acceptance means that the speaker denies either that the act happened or that they are responsible for the act.

Justification involves the speaker giving reasons that they should not be considered to be at fault. Justification differs from explanation because in the case of explanation, the speaker accepts some or all of the responsibility and asks the listener for forgiveness.

Shifting blame is a strategy that a speaker uses to avoid admitting they were wrong by suggesting that someone else should be blamed.

Table 7 shows the most common indirect phrases for making non-apologies and examples.

Table 7. Common Indirect Phrases Used in Non-Apologies

Type	Expression	Example
non-acceptance	...not on (me) ... / not my fault	Your test score is **not on me**!
	I would never...	**I would never** miss a question like that.
justification	...take into consideration... the fact that...	You're not **taking into consideration the fact that** I only had two days to do the assignment.
	...bound to happen...	With my busy schedule, this was **bound to happen**.
shifting blame	What about...	Yes, I am in charge of payments, but **what about** George, who is in charge of ordering?
	(person) is the one (who) ...	**You're the one who** told me not to come after 11 a.m.

> Recognizing the difference between an apology and a non-apology is important for predicting what a speaker will do next. Apologies signal that the speaker will change their behavior, but non-apologies signal that the speaker will not.

Comprehensive Example

 Listen to the audio file on the Pathways Website!

Look at the example conversations and notice the examples of indirect language (in **bold**). Listen to the lecture by downloading the audio file from www.pathwaystoacademicenglish.com and then answer the questions.

Example Conversation 1

MAN: **I hate to ask**, but **do you think** you could practice elsewhere?

WOMAN: Oops, I **didn't mean to** bother you. **How about** the hallway? That **should** be far enough away.

1) What is the woman likely to do next?

(A) Practice in the hallway

(B) Help the man move into the hallway

(C) Continue practicing where she is

(D) Stop practicing

Example Conversation 2

WOMAN: Oh no! I have to do better on my next test...

MAN: **Why don't you** join my study group?

WOMAN: **I'm not sure** that's a good idea. I tried it earlier in the year, but most of the members **seemed kind of** unserious, and I didn't do well on that test either.

MAN: I'm sorry, but that's **not my fault**. It was **bound to happen** with people like John in the group. He's since left though, so **if I were you**, I'd give it another chance.

WOMAN: Hmmm...**I already** told Jane I'd join her group though...

2) What can be inferred from the above discussion?

(A) The man feels responsible for the woman's poor test score.

(B) The woman will probably join the man's study group.

(C) The man wants John to rejoin the study group.

(D) The woman feels that the man's study group is not serious enough.

Explanation:

In the first example, the woman sincerely apologizes and offers to remedy the situation by moving to the hall, so we can assume that she will change her behavior accordingly. In the second example, the man makes a suggestion (not a request), but the woman refuses him twice. The man sympathizes with her situation but does not sincerely apologize.

See Page 121 for Answers

14. Tone of Voice

Tone of voice refers to how speakers use the **intonation** and **volume** of their voice to express their **intent** and add **implied meaning** to their words. Listeners, then, can **infer** whether a speaker's words are to be understood **literally**, **figuratively**, **directly**, **indirectly**, seriously, humorously, casually, formally, and so on. Therefore, learners who become familiar with how **tone of voice** is used in English will increase their listening comprehension skills.

Recognizing tone of voice helps listeners:

1. Better understand a speaker's **implied meaning**
2. Correctly **infer** a speaker's intent

For more information understanding implied meanings, see Chapters 9, 10, and 13.

To understand how tone of voice affects implied meaning, it is important to become aware of some of the functions of tone of voice. Tone of voice can:

1. Express attitude, feeling, or mood
2. Signal figurative language
3. Convey implied suggestions, disbelief, and assumptions
4. Add emphasis, politeness, and clarity
5. Indicate questions

Changes to Tone of Voice

There are various ways in which speakers can use intonation and volume to change their tone of voice. The three main ways are:

1. **Stress** – Adding emphasis to an entire word by increasing the volume.
2. **Elongating** – Adding length to the duration of vowel sounds.
3. **Pitch** – Adding rising or falling tones to words and phrases to express implied meanings.

Pitch and Attitude

Rising and falling pitch can be used to mark important words, such as the final word in a list, or to indicate that a speaker is asking a question. For example, consider the following sentence:

You went.

If speakers pronounce the words in the above sentence with a flat pitch, they are not conveying special intent; they are simply making a factual statement. However, if they raise the pitch on the word went, the speakers can convey that their intent was to ask a question.

Pitch also provides clues about a speaker's attitude towards a statement, word, or the general situation. Speakers use a falling or lower pitch when they pronounce words that they feel negatively towards, or to express displeasure. Conversely, speakers use a rising or higher pitch with words that they feel positively towards, or to express excitement, enthusiasm, or happiness.

Recognizing these patterns allows a listener to interpret what the speaker wants to say. For example, consider the following sentence:

Oh, you got a blue coat.

- If the entire sentence is said in a flat pitch, we can assume the speaker is simply noticing that the coat is blue but feels neutral about the color.
- If the speaker uses a falling pitch on the word *blue*, we would assume that the speaker is unhappy about the coat because they feel negatively about the color, specifically.
- If the speaker uses a higher or rising tone with the word *blue*, we would think that the speaker was happy about the color of the coat.

Stress and Elongating as Signals of Figurative Language

If stress or elongating is used, it often signals that the word or phrase is taking a figurative meaning (i.e., a secondary, less common, or indirect meaning).

Language in Action:
Imagine that you invited someone to a party, and their response was "I could go." If the speaker uses stress or elongation on the word *could*, it indicates that they are using the less common or metaphorical meaning (i.e., *probably not*), and thus trying to refuse the invitation. The same is true for other words that show uncertainty, such as *I don't know*, as exemplified below:

> MAN: Will you help Professor Tanaka with his research project?
>
> WOMAN: I don't know. (The woman is not sure; perhaps she has not been asked or is considering whether or not she will.)
>
> WOMAN: I don't **knooooow**. (She probably will not help or that does not want to.)

Refer to Chapter 10 for information regarding the multiple meanings of *could* and other modal verbs.

- **Exaggeration:** to describe something as bigger, better, worse, or more important than it actually is.
- **Sarcasm:** when the speaker's words should be understood to have the meaning opposite to their literal meaning.

The following are examples:

🔊 He drank *100 liters* of water after the race! (Exaggeration; he drank a lot of water.)

🔊 That's a *greeeaaaat* idea. (Sarcasm; the speaker thinks it is a bad idea.)

> Exaggeration and sarcasm are often used in speaking, particularly in conversations. However, they are rarely used in academic writing because without tone of voice to mark them, they can cause confusion.

Stress and Implied Meaning

Tone of voice can also be used to **imply** meaning. It can be used to mark words or phrases that carry **additional meaning**, without the speaker explicitly stating it. Though the additional meaning conveyed depends on the context of the statement, listening for stress can help you to understand the implied meaning.

In positive sentences, the implication is that the stressed word, and not some other one, is true, which often signals that the speaker previously misunderstood something about the word or is surprised by that particular piece of information.

In the example, *You walked to the store*, the speaker may have misheard who had walked to the store or have been confused or surprised about who had performed the action.

🔊 *Table 1. Implied Meaning via Stress in Positive Statements*

Sentence	Implication
You walked to the store.	(none)
You walked to the store.	You walked to the store – not any other person.
You *walked* to the store.	You walked to the store – you did not go by any other means of transportation.
You walked to the *store*.	You walked to the store – not to any other location.

In <u>negative sentences</u>, the stressed word indicates exactly what makes the sentence false. We can assume the other parts of the sentence are true.

In the example, *I don't want a book*, the speaker indicates that the facts in this statement are true, except for the information conveyed by the stressed word (i.e., the person who wants it). Therefore, we can assume that someone wants a book, but the speaker personally does not want it.

◀)) *Table 2. Implied Meaning via Stress in Negative Statements*

Sentence	Implication
I don't want a book.	(none)
I don't want a book.	Someone else wants a book, not the speaker.
I don't want *a* book.	The speaker wants books, not just one book.
I don't want a *book*.	The speaker wants something, but not a book.

In <u>positive questions</u>, the stressed word indicates the focus of the speaker's implied meaning. Speakers use stress to confirm or clarify information that they may or may not have received.

In the example, *What is in the blue bag?*, the speaker has probably already received some other information about the bag's contents, but wants to confirm or clarify because the answer was not heard properly, or the answer was somewhat unbelievable.

◀)) *Table 3. Implied Meaning via Stress in Positive Questions*

Sentence	Implication
What is in the blue bag?	(none)
What is in the blue bag?	Other information was received, but not exactly what the contents are.
What is *in* the blue bag?	Information was received about what is outside the bag, but not inside.
What is in the *blue* bag?	Information was received about what is inside another bag, but not the blue one.
What is in the blue *bag*?	Information was received about what is inside something blue, but not the blue bag.

In <u>negative questions</u>, the stressed word also indicates the focus of the speaker's implied meaning. However, speakers sometimes use this stress to express their assumptions or beliefs about the situation.

In the example, *Why don't you help **me**?*, the speaker assumes that the listener helps others but does not help the speaker, in particular. Similarly, in the example *Why don't **you** help me?*, the speaker believes that others help, but that only the listener, in particular, does not.

 Table 4. Implied Meaning via Stress in Negative Questions

Sentence	Implication
Why don't you help me?	(none)
Why don't *you* help me?	Others help me, but only you do not.
Why don't you help *me*?	You help others, but not me.
Why don't *you* help *me*?	I often help you, but you never help me.
Why don't you *help* me?	You do other things but never help.

Comprehensive Example

Listen to the audio file on the Pathways Website!

Look at the example conversation and notice the examples of tone of voice (in **bold**). Listen to the conversation by downloading the audio file from www.pathwaystoacademic english.com and then answer the questions.

Example Conversation

WOMAN: Do you want to work on the homework assignment together?

MAN: *Again*?! You shouldn't ask me all the time. You will never pass the test if *you* don't do your homework sometimes.

WOMAN: I don't ask *all of the time*.

---

1) Why does the man not want to help the woman?

    (A) He thinks she should try doing the homework by herself.

    (B) He thinks she should study harder.

    (C) He is tired because he already finished the homework by himself.

    (D) He does not have time.

2) What can be inferred about the woman?

    (A) She often turns in her homework late.

    (B) She never does her homework.

    (C) She often studies together with others.

    (D) She will never pass the test.

Explanation:

The man adds emphasis to the word *again* with stress, implying that the woman asks him often, and has a **cold** or **unhappy** tone of voice. He also adds stress to the word *you* in a **negative statement**, which implies that her homework gets done, but due to other people's efforts, not the woman's. The woman adds stress to the phrase *all of the time* in a **negative statement** to indicate that though she admits she often asks for help, it is not 100% of the time. Therefore, it is reasonable to assume that the woman often asks for help, even though it is not every time.

See Page 121 for Answers

15. Fluency and Pronunciation

Being able to speak competently about a topic requires a certain degree of fluency and pronunciation accuracy. **Fluency** is how long you can speak without pausing or taking breaks when presenting your ideas. **Pronunciation** accuracy relates to how well you can create both individual sounds and groups of sounds. Speakers who pause too frequently or for too long and have poor pronunciation are difficult for listeners to understand.

> Fluency and pronunciation are required for several different speaking tasks, including orally summarizing from notes (Chapter 6), stating opinions (Chapter 8), and discussing academic topics (Chapter 16).

Improving Fluency

To improve fluency, you need to monitor your speaking speed and know what to do when your speech breaks down.

Practice helps learners to use expressions fluently. One way to practice is through individual speaking exercises, using the following steps:

1. Learn set expressions such as those given in previous chapters.
2. Try to speak at length about various topics with little to no preparation, using the set expressions.
3. Speak about the same topics, focusing on speaking more than in previous attempts.
4. Speak about the same topics, focusing on speaking more quickly than in previous attempts. Use a word-counter and stop-watch to monitor your speaking speed.

> See Chapters 6, 8, and 16 for lists of set expressions that are useful in various situations.

> To check your spoken fluency, choose a topic and try to speak about it for a set amount of time, such as one or two minutes. Record the speech and transcribe it using a computer. Count the number of words and divide by the number of minutes to find your average rate of words spoken per minute. Although this is not a perfect measurement of fluency, you can use it to check how fluent you are and to aim for improvement. Attempt this task every few weeks and try to improve your average rate of words spoken per minute.

Speaking more quickly does not mean changing your pace when saying individual words. You should also focus on how much time is spent pausing. One way to decrease the time spent pausing is to use fillers.

Fillers are words or phrases that help maintain the conversation and signal to the listener that the speaker is not yet finished speaking but is instead thinking of what to say next. Although words such as *uh…* or *umm…* can be used, they are not well-respected in academic English, so consider trying some of the following fillers instead.

Table 1. Common Fillers

…the thing is…	…(what) I mean (is) …	well…
what I'm trying to say is…	it turns out that…	let me see…

> Use fillers and repeats to naturally fill the pauses in your speech. Simply repeating what you have already said or restarting allows you to continue talking without leaving a long silence that makes the listener wonder if you have finished speaking.

Consider the following two short oral reports about a topic, one with fillers and repeats and one without. Notice that the second report contains fillers and repeats and has fewer pauses and more words. This makes it easier for the listener to follow and understand that the speaker is not yet finished.

1. I will talk about the school's policy of adding more online classes… in my opinion… it is a good idea… because… because it will make more… classes available to students.

2. I will talk about the school's policy of adding more online classes. **Let me see.** **Well**, in my opinion, it is a good idea. **What I'm trying to say is**, it is a good idea because it will make more classes. **The thing is**, more classes means more available classes for students, so I think it is a good idea.

Improving Pronunciation Accuracy

Below are some common difficulties that Japanese learners have when learning English pronunciation that you should practice.

1. Individual Sounds

In general, Japanese has fewer sounds than English. Many Japanese learners of English tend to confuse two different English sounds and pronounce them the same or similarly. Look at the list of commonly confused sounds in Table 2 and check that you can pronounce and hear the differences between them.

Table 2. Often Confused Similar Sounds

Sound 1	Sound 2
r (e.g., *pray*)	l (e.g., *play*)
b (e.g., *ban*)	v (e.g., *van*)
s (e.g., *sing*)	th (e.g., *thing*)
shi (e.g., *shine*)	si (e.g., *sign*)
z (e.g., *zen*)	th (e.g., *then*)
a (e.g., *hat*)	u (e.g., *hut*)
ee (e.g., *been*)	i (e.g., *bin*)
o (e.g., *not*)	o (e.g., *note*)

> Be aware that there are some differences in various English dialects. For example, vowel sounds are pronounced differently in British and American English. Listen to a variety of English accents to become familiar with any differences in pronunciation.

2. Phonemic Stress

Some syllables in a word receive more stress than others. This is called **phonemic stress**. In English, phonemic stress can result in a change in vowel sound, and some words even have two different phonemic stresses depending on whether they are being used as a verb or a noun. Because this stress can change the meaning of a sentence, it is important to understand the basic concepts related to phonemic stress. Below are some general guidelines.

1. For two-syllable words, nouns and adjectives are usually stressed on the first syllable, whereas verbs are generally stressed on the second syllable.

    (E.g.) EXport = noun; exPORT = verb

    REcord = noun; reCORD = verb

2. Words ending with the suffixes (see Chapter 1) -*ic*, -*tion*, and -*ity* usually place stress on the syllable just before the suffix.

    (E.g.) aMORPHic, hisTORic, evaluAtion, conDItion, inaBILity

3. Words ending with the suffixes -*al*, and -*y* usually place stress on the third syllable from the end.

> (E.g.) conSENsual, biOlogy

3. Linking

Linking is when two separate words are blended together when they are pronounced. Well-known examples include contractions such as *you're* (you are) and *I'm* (I am).

There are also several instances when linking occurs in pronunciation but not in writing such as:

- You-linking
- Of-linking
- Common sound linking
- Consonant-vowel linking

You-linking occurs when the word *you* appears after a word ending in a consonant, resulting in a blend, similar to the *y-* blends in Japanese. Consider the following examples.

Blend	Example	Linked Pronunciation
d + you = ju	Would you...	Wou**ju**...
t + you = chu	I know what you...	I know wha**chu**...
n + you = nyu	Can you...	Ca**nyu**...

Of-linking is used with the word *of* and results in *of* being blended with the previous word and pronounced as a *uh-* sound. This is often spelled with *a* in colloquial English (*lotta, outta, etc.*). Consider the following examples.

a lot of money   → a **lott(uh)** money

out of town   →   **out(uh)** town

some of these   →   **some(uh)** these

Common sound linking occurs when a word begins with the consonant sound that the previous word ended with. In this case, the words are linked and pronounced as one. This occurs as long as the two consonant sounds are the same, even if the letter used to spell the sound differs across the two words. Consider the following examples.

first time   →   firs_**t**ime

it's so   →   it**s**_**o**

black coffee   →   bla_**c**offee

Consonant-vowel linking occurs when a word that begins with a vowel appears after a word that ends in a consonant. Also, in some dialects of English, if the consonant is a *t* sound, it becomes voiced, causing it to be pronounced like a *d*. Consider the following examples.

The plane just took off	→	The plane just too_k**o**ff.
He looks up to his brother	→	He loo_**ks**up to his brother.
I bought it yesterday	→	I bou_**d**it yesterday

4. Reduction

Reduction is when certain sounds are simply not pronounced at all. The following are some of the most common reductions in spoken English.

 Table 3. Common Pronunciation Reductions in English

Reduction	Example
he, him, her → 'e, 'im, 'er	What did **he** want? → What did 'e want?
going to → gonna	I'm **going to** visit Australia. → I'm **gonna** visit Australia.
have to → hafta	I **have to** go now. → I **hafta** go now.
has to → hasta	He **has to** get a job. → He **hasta** get a job.
give me → gimme	**Give me** three of those. → **Gimme** three of those.
and → 'n	I like salt **and** pepper. → I like salt **'n** pepper.
are → 're	Mom and Dad **are** coming. → Mom and Dad**'re** coming.

5. Rhythm and Stress

In stress-based languages such as English, the duration of an utterance's pronunciation depends on whether it is a content word or a function word.

- **Content words** (nouns, verbs, adjectives, adverbs, demonstrative pronouns, interrogative adverbs, etc.) are pronounced longer because they contain important meaning for the sentence.
- **Function words** are words that have grammatical significance but carry little meaning (e.g., auxiliary verbs such as *have* and grammatical prepositions such as *to*) and are pronounced more quickly.

Consider the following sentence. Note that more stress is placed on the content words, in **bold**, and that they are pronounced for a longer duration than the function words.

(E.g.) **Help Mike carry all** of the **boxes** to the **attic**.

In general, function words and unstressed syllables will be either linked, reduced, or spoken more quickly in order to maintain a basic number of stressed syllables per second, which creates **rhythm**.

Consider the following example sentences, which get progressively longer but contain the same number of content words. They will all be pronounced in the same amount of time.

Dogs hate cats.

My **dogs hate cats**. → (my) dogs hate cats.

My **dogs hate** your **cats**. → (my) dogs hacher cats.

My **dogs** will **hate** your **cats**. → (my) dogs'll hacher cats.

My **dogs** are going to **hate** your **cats**. → (my) dogs're gonna hacher cats.

In the examples above, the pronunciation of the stressed content words and unstressed syllables creates a rhythm, similar to that of music. The stressed syllables are like whole notes, whereas the unstressed syllables are like half or quarter notes that are compressed to fit within the same amount of time. Notice that although the total number of syllables in each of the phrases differs, the amount of time needed to produce them remains the same.

Mastering linking, reduction, and rhythm will also improve your fluency.

Comprehensive Example

Listen to the audio file on the Pathways Website!

Look at the example responses to the question "What is an appropriate amount of sleep for a university student to get each night?" Notice that the first example makes little use of fillers, repeats, stress and rhythm. Listen to the audio file and then try to match the pronunciation and rhythm of the second example.

Example 1

An appropriate amount... of sleep for... university students... is about six hours... each night because... it is healthiest.

Example 2

An appropriate amount(**u**) sleep for university student**s_is**, **well**, about six hours. **It_turns_o**ut that six hours(**u**) slee**p_is** good because, **the thing_is**, it_is very healthy for students. **What_I mean_is** that anything less than six hour**s_is** unhealthy.

16. Discussion Strategies

Discussing academic topics involves asking questions, getting information, and exchanging ideas about study or research related topics.

> Developing discussion strategies and learning the expressions in this chapter will help you to successfully obtain information and efficiently exchange ideas with others.

Having a discussion is different from having a casual conversation because there is usually some purpose to a discussion. An academic discussion often requires that <u>all</u> participants give their ideas and opinions and compare these to those of others. A discussion usually ends when a decision has been reached or all parties have received all of the information that they wanted.

In order to participate in discussions, you must be able to:
- Recognize a variety of greetings
- Ask questions and give opinions
- Open a discussion
- Show interest in what others are saying
- Ask others for their opinions
- Ask for repetition and clarification
- Disagree
- Direct the discussion

> Review Chapter 8 for information about forming questions, responding to greetings, and giving opinions effectively.

Opening a Discussion

When several people participate in a discussion, it is important to clarify what will be discussed and to define the topic. Below are some common phrases to open a discussion and an example.

Table 1. Phrases for Opening a Discussion

Today, we need to…	The reason we're meeting is…	Let's begin by…

Each year, millions of people suffer from a circadian rhythm problem called Seasonal Affective Disorder, or SAD. **Today, we need to** discuss what causes SAD and how we can prevent it.

Showing Interest in What Others Say

When participating in a discussion, it is important to be an active group member. This means offering responses, and often following them up with questions. Below are some common phrases for offering quick responses and examples of how to use them in a conversation.

Table 2. Phrases for Quick Response

Really?!	You're kidding!	Oh no! / Oh, right!
That's an interesting point.	I see what you mean.	That makes sense.

A: Engineers are closer than ever to making huge advances in aerodynamics. By learning how to manipulate invisible aerodynamic drag forces, inventors will soon be able to develop incredibly fuel-efficient modes of transportation.

B: **Really?! That's an interesting** development. I think we should put more money into researching this area. How much fuel do you think can be saved?

Asking Others for Their Opinions

In order to have an effective discussion, input is needed from all participants, whether the discussion is taking place between two people or within a small group. When there are participants in a discussion who have not yet spoken, other participants should prompt them to speak. Below are some common phrases to encourage others to offer their opinions and an example.

Table 3. Phrases for Asking Others for Their Opinions

What do you think about...	What are your first thoughts on...	Do you have any ideas?

A: I heard that researchers have developed a method for the rapid 3D printing of fully functional electronic circuits. **What are your first thoughts on** this, John?

B: Well... I think it will be great for the electronics manufacturing industry, as it will allow companies to mass-produce fully functional components.

Asking for Repetition and Clarification

When a participant in a discussion fails to understand what a speaker says, it helps to ask the speaker to repeat, clarify, or paraphrase what was said. Below are some common phrases to ask for repetition and clarification and an example.

Table 4. Phrases for Asking for Repetition and Clarification

What do you mean (by that)?	Can you be more specific?	What are you saying?
Can you give me more details?	I can't understand why/how…?	Are you saying that…?

A: I want you to take a look at the satellite image of this small island and give me an estimate of its circumference in kilometers.

B: I'm sorry, I don't understand what you mean. **Can you be more specific?**

A: Sure. Look carefully at this satellite photo. What do you think is the total distance around the island? If you were to walk completely around it, how many kilometers do you think you would walk?

Disagreeing

Disagreements are a natural part of a discussion. However, speakers should be careful not to be too rude or offensive when disagreeing.

Refer Chapter 13 to review ways to be polite and avoid offending others.

One way to avoid being rude in a discussion is to indicate appreciation for the other person's idea or argument before offering a **counterpoint**. Below are some common phrases to appreciate others' ideas and an example. Note that these phrases generally must be followed by a word or phrase that indicates a counterpoint such as *but*, *however*, or *although*.

Table 5. Phrases for Appreciating Others' Ideas

You're making a good point	I appreciate what you're saying	You're right about…

A: It's my opinion that the abuse of public power for private gain cannot be eradicated. History has proven again and again that corruption and abuse of power are present within all societies. People will always act in their own best interests at the expense of others.

B: **You're making a good point. However**, I'm not sure if I completely agree. I would argue that there are examples of utopian societies in history, which suggest that there is hope for a corruption-free civilization.

Notice how Speaker B uses phrases of uncertainty and hedging (i.e., *I'm not sure, completely*) to increase indirectness and politeness.

Directing a Discussion

When having a group discussion, it is sometimes necessary to **direct the discussion** to other topics, or to return to a topic if some members begin talking about unrelated matters. Below are some common phrases to direct the discussion back to an original topic or to a new topic and an example.

Table 6. Phrases for Directing a Discussion

Getting back to the point...	Wait (just) a minute.	Anyway...
Speaking of (which)...	If there are no other ideas...	Let's move on.

A: I think we need to ask Professor Smith for more funds in order to finish the current project.

B: **Speaking of the project**, should we change the timeline? I think there is too much work to finish by January.

A: **Wait just a minute**. I would like to decide what to do about funding first. Do we all agree that we need to request more funds?

> Notice how Speaker B attempts to direct the discussion to a new topic (i.e., *the timeline of the project*), but speaker A directs the discussion back to the original topic (i.e., *funding for the project*) because a decision has not been reached.

Comprehensive Example

 Listen to the audio file on the Pathways Website!

Look at the sample discussions and listen to the audio file. Notice how the set phrases from this chapter, in **bold**, are used in the discussions.

Discussion 1: Two Person Discussion

JESSICA: Nick, what's up?
   NICK: Oh, nothing much, you?
JESSICA: The same. So, did you do the homework for Professor Anderson's class yet?
   NICK: Yeah.
JESSICA: Well, I was wondering if you wanted to compare answers. I thought number 5 was really difficult.
   NICK: I guess so.

JESSICA: **What do you mean**?

NICK: It wasn't so bad. I mean, I finished.

JESSICA: Yeah, but just because you finished doesn't mean it was easy. Do you know what I mean?

NICK: Well, I thought some of the problems were difficult, like number 1. At first, I thought it was easy, but then I realized we also had to calculate the amount of friction.

JESSICA: But what about number 5?

NICK: **Oh, right!** I don't think that one was so bad. It was pretty straightforward.

JESSICA: **I can't understand why** you think it was straightforward.

NICK: **Really?!** Professor Anderson did a similar problem on the board at the end of class.

JESSICA: **That makes sense**… I had to leave early for a doctor's appointment. Do you think you could show me how to solve it?

NICK: No problem! Why don't we meet at the library later?

Discussion 2: Group Discussion

STACEY: Hi everyone, how's everything?

JASON: Alright.

MARY: I can't complain.

STACEY: Okay, **the reason we're meeting is** to decide how to use the extra funds left over from the budget. Jason, **do you have any ideas**?

JASON: Why don't we buy an extra camera? We could really use a second one, and there's no telling when the first one will break.

STACEY: **That makes sense.** How about you, Mary? **Do you have any ideas**?

MARY: I think we should just return the money to the university.

STACEY: **Really?! What are you saying?**

MARY: Well, we're not supposed to use money from the budget unless it is absolutely necessary for club activities and there is a penalty for using them inappropriately.

STACEY: **Are you saying that** you think buying a second camera is an inappropriate use of the funds?

MARY: Actually, I don't think it's inappropriate, but what if the university thinks it is? Can we really justify buying another camera when the first one works just fine?

STACEY: **I see what you mean.** Jason, do you think we can make a good enough argument to buy a second camera?

JASON: That's no problem! The official university rules say that a club can purchase up to three cameras, and we currently only have one. Also, having a second one will allow us to edit the video, which is important for our club activities. Several other clubs have multiple cameras and they haven't received any penalties.

MARY: **Really?!** Well... if you don't think we'll get in any trouble for it, I am not against buying a second camera.

STACEY: So, we all agree that getting a second camera is a good use of the funds. **If there are no other ideas**, why don't we stop for today?

JASON: Sounds good to me!

Comprehensive Examples Answers

Chapter 1:

1) C   2) D   3) A

Chapter 2:

1) B   2) C   3) A   4) B   5) D

Chapter 3:

1) A   2) C   3) D   4) B   5) C

Chapter 7:

1) C   2) A   3) D   4) C   5) D

Chapter 9:

1) D   2) B

Chapter 10:

1) C   2) D

Chapter 11:

1) B   2) B   3) A

Chapter 13:

1) A   2) D

Chapter 14:

1) A   2) C

Use the online tools found on the Pathways Website for more practice!

編 集

Ryan Spring

Vincent Scura

執 筆

Barry Kavanagh

Yoshio Kitahara

Richard Meres

Takayuki Miura

Sachiko Nakamura

Shizuka Sakurai

Vincent Scura

Ryan Spring

Shuichi Takebayashi

Jessica Takeda

表紙デザイン

Nami Ogata

Jessica Takeda

Pathways to Academic English 4th Edition, v2

©Institute for Excellence in Higher Education, Tohoku University 2024

2024 年 2 月 9 日　初版第 1 刷発行

編　者／東北大学高度教養教育・学生支援機構
発行者／関　内　　隆
発行所／東北大学出版会
　　　　〒 980-8577　仙台市青葉区片平 2-1-1
　　　　TEL：022-214-2777　FAX：022-214-2778
　　　　https://www.tups.jp　E-mail：info@tups.jp
印　刷／株式会社 センキョウ
　　　　〒 983-0035　仙台市宮城野区日の出町二丁目 4-2
　　　　TEL：022-236-7161